PEARL HARBOR

50th ANNIVERSARY SPECIAL EDITION

PEARL HARBOR

50TH ANNIVERSARY SPECIAL EDITION

The Associated Press

Written by Sid Moody

Additional text by Hugh A. Mulligan
Edited by Norm Goldstein
Photo Research by Susan Brady

Longmeadow Press

Published by Longmeadow Press, 201 High Ridge Road, Stamford, CT 06904.

Cover design by Brenda McGee/David Merrell
Interior design by Allan Mogel

ISBN: 0-681-41409-X
Printed in U.S.A.

0 9 8 7 6 5 4 3

CONTENTS

1
TUFFY LEEMANS DAY

With several Japanese flags below the canopy, this P-40 sits at the entrance of Wheeler Field, Oahu, scene of the devastating attack on the old Army Air Corps during December 7, 1941.

As if not to awaken the slumbering Americans, Commander Gishiro Mirua padded about the carrier Akagi in slippers.

The practice more befitted a houseboy than the navigator of a flagship of *kido butai* — striking force. Yet Mirua bore an immense burden — not to say when but certainly from where the Japanese force would strike.

Towards evening, Mirua did his arcane calculation to the line that stretched some forty–five hundred miles across the Pacific. It ended here, just so. Latitude 25 degrees, 2 minutes north. Longitude 157 degrees, 58 minutes west.

He relayed his calculations on to Admiral Chuichi Nagumo, commander of *kido butai*. Nagumo signalled his warships to slow engines. Oil was a precious commodity — five–gallon tins of it were stowed in every nook and cranny — and the ships were on an empty sea so far from home.

At almost the same time two hundred and twenty miles due south, Santa Claus came in for a landing at Kapiolani Park to the delight of small fry on Oahu in the Hawaiian Islands. Instead of a sled and reindeer, Santa arrived in a plane on loan from the 86th Bombardment Squadron.

Christmastime, December 6, 1941.

Thus stood two worlds apart, about to be fused in war.

* * * * *

The surprising thing about the surprise *kido butai* was poised to deliver upon Pearl Harbor in Oahu was that it was a surprise. The Japanese codes that Americans had broken and had been reading for months left little doubt that the Japanese were going to attack somewhere momentarily. The air was filled with revealing traffic, what radio people call "noise." But there was no one place where

View of the city and harbor of Honolulu before the attack. Markers in the foreground give distances to distant cities. The marker on left gives the mileage to Wellington, New Zealand.

all the noise was collected and analyzed. The pieces of noise were not put together to solve the puzzle.

Furthermore, America felt safe behind the barrier of its two oceans. Pearl Harbor was impregnable, the Gibraltar of the Pacific. The United States was also deluded by an implied racism. Aggressive and duplicitous they may be, but the Japanese were no match for Uncle Sam. They might be able to manhandle the Chinese, but they'd never come up against American boys. A paper tiger.

On the eve of learning otherwise, the United States was in a schizoid state. Part of it wanted to stay out of any war, across the Pacific or Atlantic. President Franklin Delano Roosevelt had gotten Lend–Lease aid to embattled Great Britain approved in March, but that fall the draft renewal had passed Congress by only one vote. The peace at any price faction was sizeable, its vitriol exceeding any definition of dovish.

In Des Moines, America's hero, Charles A. Lindbergh, proclaimed to a sympathetic audience of America Firsters: "The British, the Jews and the

Roosevelt Administration are the three most important groups who have been pressing this country toward war."

On the day after Santa's visit to Honolulu, seven hundred Jews were herded into trucks near the Polish town of Chelmno. The doors were locked and sealed by German guards. Then the motors were started and the exhaust piped into the back of the trucks. It was the first such experimental execution by the Nazis.

At Princeton University, students facetiously asked Roosevelt to name an unknown soldier of the next war "so we can know who he is before he gets killed."

That October 17, south of Iceland, the U.S. destroyer Kearney was damaged by a German U–boat torpedo while escorting a Lend–Lease convoy to Britain. Eleven sailors were killed.

Sunday, December 7, Pennsylvania Senator Charlie Sipes was to tell a roaring America First crowd at Soldiers' and Sailors' Memorial Hall in Pittsburgh: "The chief warmonger in the United States, to my way of thinking, is the president of the United States!"

On October 31, another destroyer, the USS Reuben James, had been torpedoed and went down with one hundred and fifteen crewmen, again off Iceland.

In Honolulu, posters greeted lei–bedecked tourists getting off the steamer Lurline promising "A World of Happiness in an Ocean of Peace."

By December, Hitler's panzers had driven to within sight of Moscow in six months. In Western Europe, Britain, having won the Battle of Britain in 1940, stood, desperately, alone. Japanese troops had driven the Chinese from their coast and in July occupied French Indo–China. France, half occupied itself by Nazi troops, was powerless to protest.

Cartoonist Milton Caniff was asked to please stop putting the Japanese red ball on enemy planes in his comic strip "Terry and the Pirates." He did.

* * * * *

That December, Americans were reading Edna Ferber's best–seller, "Saratoga Trunk," at $2.50 a copy. For 55 cents, they could get a matinee seat on Broadway to see Lillian Hellman's anti–Nazi play, "Watch on the Rhine." For $38 you could buy an expensive suit at Rogers Peet in New York. Or "miracle" nylons for $1.65.

Against the "noise" of such everyday facts of life, Roosevelt was trying to cajole a reluctant, isolationist nation into his belief that the world's wars would

An airview of Honolulu before December 7, 1941.

eventually reach it. After consultation with the British, the American military had decided that the war in Europe was its first concern and anything that might eventuate in the Pacific, second. But the nation was ill prepared for either.

The technological marvel of radar, which for the first time gave commanders battlefield vision beyond the horizon, had just been developed. Since Thanksgiving, five sets had been stationed on Hawaii, one at Kahuku Point on the northernmost part of Oahu. The Army had asked permission to put them atop high points where they could see farthest. Governor John Poindexter and the National Park Service refused. They would blemish the landscape.

Lieutenant General Walter C. Short, Army commander in Hawaii, thought the best use of radar, for the moment, was for training. Nonetheless, after receiving a "war warning" from Washington on November 28, Short had the sets fire up at 4 a.m. instead of 6. They were to stay on until 7 a.m. Short thought dawn the most dangerous time for any attack.

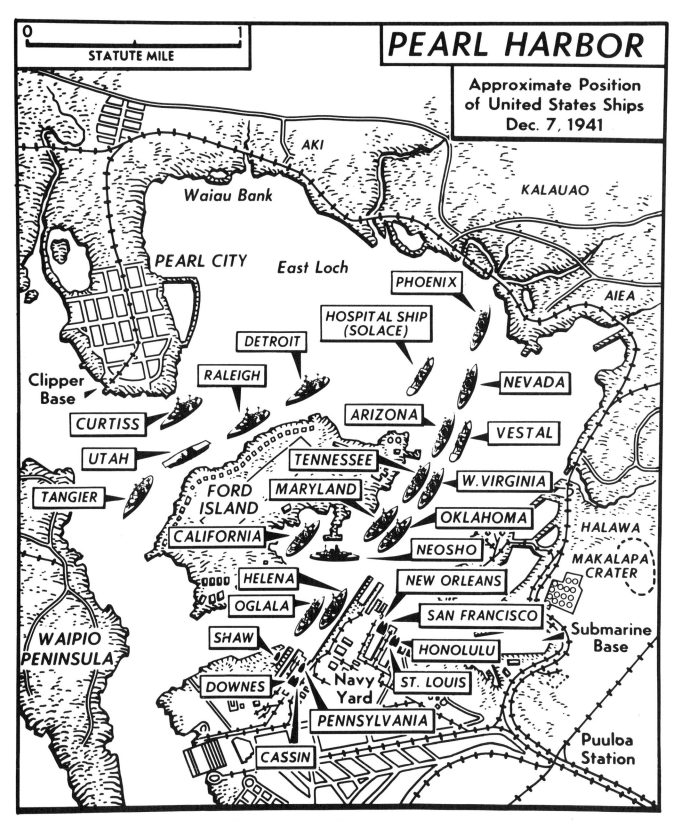

STATUTE MILE

PEARL HARBOR

Approximate Position
of United States Ships
Dec. 7, 1941

AKI

KALAUAO

Waiau Bank

PEARL CITY

East Loch

AIEA

PHOENIX

HOSPITAL SHIP (SOLACE)

DETROIT

RALEIGH

Clipper Base

NEVADA

ARIZONA

VESTAL

CURTISS

UTAH

TENNESSEE

W. VIRGINIA

MARYLAND

HALAWA

TANGIER

FORD ISLAND

OKLAHOMA

MAKALAPA CRATER

CALIFORNIA

NEOSHO

HELENA

NEW ORLEANS

OGLALA

SAN FRANCISCO

Submarine Base

WAIPIO PENINSULA

SHAW

HONOLULU

DOWNES

Navy Yard

ST. LOUIS

PENNSYLVANIA

Puuloa Station

CASSIN

This map of Pearl Harbor shows U.S. Navy capital ships in positions based on approximate positions of the same units as shown in the Navy map which was among exhibits at opening session of the congressional committee investigating the 1941 disaster.

While Short's primary duty was to protect the huge Pearl Harbor naval installation, his real worry was potential sabotage from the 157,905 residents of Japanese blood in the islands. One–quarter of the first generation immigrants were still Japanese citizens. Two–thirds of the *nisei,* or second generation, had dual citizenship. As a safeguard, he had his Army Air Corps fighters, including ninety top-line P-40s, disarmed and bunched together so they could be guarded more easily against saboteurs. He did the same with his Flying Fortresses, the four–engined B–17 bombers.

A lineup of Japanese light cruisers on maneuvers.

The Army anti–aircraft unit that protected Ford Island in the middle of Pearl Harbor was actually stationed fifteen miles and a ferry ride away at Camp Malakole. Daily they carted the guns in and reassembled them. On December 7 the men were given a day off. Indeed, only one–quarter of the anti-aircraft guns at Pearl Harbor were manned, only four of the Army's thirty-one batteries. For fear of sabotage and because it "was apt to disintegrate and get dusty," the ammunition was in storage under lock and key. It was often hard to find who had the keys. Particularly on weekends.

Short's counterpart, Admiral Husband E. Kimmel, commander of the Pacific Fleet, had also cut down the daily three-hundred-mile patrols set up by his predecessor, Admiral James O. Richardson. The pilots protested that flying seven days a week was wearing out them and their sixty PBY Catalinas.

When Army fighters buzzed a ceremonial aloha as the steamer Lurline left Honolulu December 3, they returned to Hickam Field where they were once again,

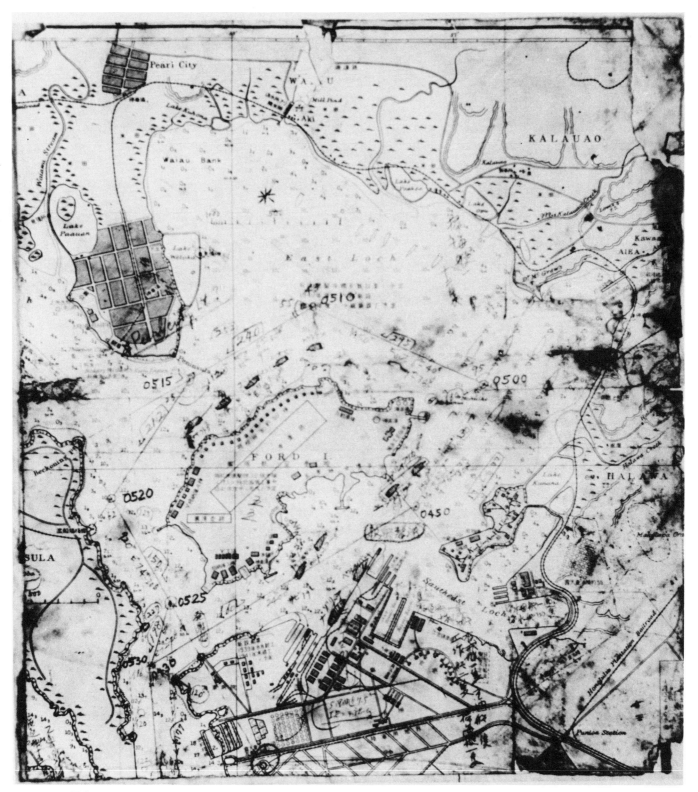

This map, released by the Navy on December 23, 1941, was described as a Pearl Harbor chart found in a captured Japanese submarine. The Navy caption said: "Japanese symbols drawn on the chart indicate the anchorage of ships and details of military establishments around the inner harbor of Pearl Harbor, U.S. Naval base in Hawaii."

bunched together. The estimate was they could be dispersed in thirty to thirty-five minutes and be gassed, armed and airborne in four hours, plenty of time after any foreseeable attack warning.

Not all heads were in the sand at Pearl Harbor. Captain Ellis Zacharias, formerly in naval intelligence and now skipper of cruiser Salt Lake City, said in November there would be no sabotage from local Japanese. "The attack would conform to their historical procedure, that of attacking before war was declared," he told a friend. Tipping off civilians in advance risked losing surprise through leaks.

It was obvious, however, as the weekend of December 7 began, that the Japanese were going to jump somewhere. And Secretary of Navy Frank Knox told a private group in Washington December 4: "The Navy is not going to be caught napping." Two days later at a Saturday meeting at the Navy Department, Knox asked his admirals: "Gentlemen, are they going to hit us?" "No, Mr. Secretary," replied Rear Admiral Richmond Kelly Turner, "they're going to hit the British. They aren't ready for us yet." Knox accepted this even though earlier he had written War Secretary Henry Stimson: "If war eventuates with Japan, it is ... easily possible that hostilities would be initiated by a surprise attack upon the fleet or the naval base at Pearl Harbor."

Early in December Kimmel had told Joseph C. Harsch of the Christian Science Monitor: "Moscow is not going to fall this winter. That means that the Japanese cannot attack us in the Pacific without running the risk of a two–front war. The Japanese are too smart to run that risk."

The evidence farther west was to the contrary. Catalinas of Admiral Thomas C. Hart's Asian Fleet in Manila had spotted on December 2nd about twenty Japanese transports and warships in Cam Ranh Bay in Indo–China. Next day there were thirty. And the next day they were all gone. On December 6 U.S. Ambassador John G. Winant sent an "urgent" to Washington from London that thirty-five transports, eight cruisers and twenty destroyers in two armadas were headed for the Kra Peninsula in British Malaya. The significance was lost but there were no carriers.

Flight Lieutenant John Lockwood of the Royal Australian Air Force had been one of the spotters from an RAAF Hudson. In fact, he got so close the Japanese shot at him. On landing he told his mates: "I'm the first to be fired on in this war." Except for millions of Chinese and, unofficially some Russians, he was right.

That same day Hart had been host to his counterpart for the British Asiatic Fleet based in Singapore, Vice Admiral Sir Tom Phillips. Hart told him unidentified planes had overflown Clark Field the last three nights. This was home base for General Douglas MacArthur's air force. Believed to be closer to any Japanese target, he had priority over Hawaii for new planes. MacArthur so far had received one hundred and seven new fighters of a promised two hundred and forty and thirty-five of one hundred and sixty-five B–17s. Phillips told Hart he'd better be getting back to Singapore and would leave the next morning, December 7, Washington time.

Said Hart: "If you want to be there when the war starts, I suggest taking off right now."

* * *

A Japanese naval aircraft carrier.

Kido butai sailed as an avenging angel to bring judgment for wrongs, real or imagined, the Empire of the Rising Sun believed had dishonored it. Paradoxically its intended victim was the very nation that brought it back into the world in 1853. Within fifty-two years of its arousal from its feudal warrior isolation, Japan had fought with all of its neighbors but one, the United States of America. Now it was rectifying that omission in a brilliantly conceived ambush — a desperate gamble, really — against America's keystone naval base at Pearl Harbor.

No one was more aware of what a gamble *kido butai* was than its brilliant creator, Admiral Isoroku Yamamoto. He had no illusions about Japan's chances in a war with the industrial power of the West. But his patriotism, his intellect, his love of gambling had all been challenged. If his more headstrong colleagues must go to war, and if they intended to do so by seizing the oil of Dutch Indonesia and

16

The Japanese battleship Haruna.

The bombers attacking Pearl Harbor took off from airplane carriers. This is the Akagi, one of Japan's largest and fastest carriers. The ship was listed as carrying fifty planes, its tonnage at 26,900.

rubber of British Malaya, then the only way to succeed was by neutralizing the might of the U.S. Navy on the Japanese flank. And the only way to do that was by surprise. It was, as it turned out, a grave miscalculation, one that Yamamoto did not live to see realized.

Commander Kikuichi Fujita of the cruiser Tone foresaw the consequences graphically: "I think this sortie is going to be like going into a tiger's lair to get her cubs."

The Japanese navy in 1941 was a first class fighting force. Its torpedo skills far exceeded that of the U.S. It excelled at night fighting. It included ten battleships including the world's two mightiest, eight aircraft carriers, thirty cruisers and one hundred and eight destroyers. At the very moment Gishiro Mirua was fine tuning his position, twenty-seven Japanese submarines ringed the Hawaiian Islands.

Nagumo, fortunately for the U.S., had little understanding of or appreciation for air power. He was a battleship man. But he spoke for many besides himself before his fleet sailed from remote Hitokappu Bay in the Kurile islands north of Japan proper, a lonely spot of a few shacks, a post office and a wireless transmitter. "This Empire is now going to war with an arrogant and predestined enemy," said the admiral. This precisely encapsulated the paranoia of Japan's ultra-nationalists.

Bombers and torpedo planes had been practicing for months, but few knew the task force's mission. To keep it vague, the crew had been issued both summer and winter clothing. Nagumo weighed anchor November 26 and headed east across the Pacific. Yamamoto's chief of staff, Admiral Matome Ugaki, confided to his diary: "It is not unfair to assault one who is sleeping. This means victory over a most careless enemy." This was in the best tradition of the *samurai*, Japan's revered feudal warrior class.

Yamamoto stayed behind in his flagship, the old but updated battleship Nagato. But he bade bon voyage to *kido butai* with the identical "Z" signal Admiral Heihachiro Togo had flown when he annihilated the Russian fleet in 1905 at the Battle of Tsushima Strait (and very similar to Horatio Nelson's at Trafalgar): "The fate of the Empire depends on this war. Do your duty."

Many admirals had resisted Yamamoto's daring plan. They thought it impossible to sail that far, even in the stormy, deserted, wintry north Pacific, without being discovered. And they worried how the fleet would be refueled. Japan's warships were designed to operate in waters much closer to home. Seven oilers and supply ships accompanied *kido butai*. Days before Nagumo sailed, other warships and transports had set out from Japan for Formosa and the

Kole Kole pass, above Schofield Barracks, with the pineapple fields in foreground.

Pescadores to stage for simultaneous surprise attacks on Malaya and the Philippines, all timed with the Pearl Harbor raid.

Kido butai's main might was its six carriers. Yamamoto's naysayers had protested putting so many eggs in one perilous basket. As well, they would be needed to cover the southbound invasion forces. All or nothing, argued Yamamoto. The carrier names reflected Japan's dualism — love of nature, admiration of the samurai — warships all yet called Kaga (Increased Joy), Soryu (Green Dragon), Shokaku (Soaring Crane), Zuikaku (Happy Crane), Akagi (Red Castle), Hiryu (Flying Dragon). The Japanese knew their prime opponent was the American carriers, bearers of proud names from the nation's military history: Lexington, Saratoga, Enterprise. In war games seven months before, Yamamoto's striking force lost two carriers and a third of its planes.

Accompanying the carriers were two battleships, two heavy cruisers and nine destroyers with a vanguard of three of Japan's biggest submarines. Nagumo was ordered to turn back if discovered before December 6, but if only part of his armada had been spotted, he was to continue on. After December 6, he was to

19

A replica of a Kyoto Byodo-in Temple in Oahu's Valley of Temples Memorial Park, which draws thousands of Japanese tourists today. It is near Kaneohe Marine base, which was a Naval air station at the time of the Pearl Harbor attack.

fight his way in. En route he was: "To sink anything carrying any flag." But the heaving sea was empty.

Kido butai kept total radio silence. Transmitter keys were removed from radios. Kazuyoshi Kochi, communications officer on battleship Hiei, put an essential part of his radio in a box and used it as a pillow. Commanders slept on the bridge, in uniform. Pilots were given photographs of their targets. Petty Officer Noboru Kanai, one of the fleet's best bombardiers sat in his plane all day practicing. (He was to be credited with a hit on the battleship Arizona.) On Akagi, pilots memorized a plaster of paris relief map of Pearl Harbor.

On December 2 Yamamoto signalled the silent fleet the final go–ahead: "Climb Mount Niitaka." Mount Niitaka was the highest point in the Japanese Empire. Revealing of what Japan had become, it was not in that nation at all. It was on Formosa, won by war with China in 1895.

At 1800 hours on December 6, *kido butai* fueled in rough seas for the last time. Sub-lieutenant Iyozo Fujita, a fighter pilot on Soryu, drank several bottles of beer. Then he took a bath so he would be as cleansed as a samurai warrior of old. He put photographs of his dead parents into his pocket and turned in.

To the south, five midget submarines were being launched from their larger mother ships. These were eighty one–foot craft carrying two torpedoes plus two crew members who each carried a pistol and a samurai sword. Not expecting to come back, the crew men had left clippings of their fingernails and some hair back at Kure to be delivered to their families. Ensign Kazuo Sakamaki fell overboard twice trying to board his bouncing craft. He clung to a bottle of perfume he had brought with him so he could smell "like cherry blossoms falling to the ground."

As Ensign Akira Hiroo cast off from submarine I–20 he told its deck crew:"The ice cream sold at Honolulu is especially fine. I will bring you some when I come back."

Back home aboard Nagato, Yamamoto played five games of Japanese chess with Commander Yasuji Watanabe. He won three of them. Then he went to his cabin. While waiting for news he composed a *waka,* a thirty-one–syllable poem:

"It is my sole wish to serve the Emperor as his shield.

"I will not spare my honor or my life."

Far to the east Sunday dawn had just begun to pearl the sky. *Kido butai* was at Gishiro Mirua's last dot on his chart of the vast ocean, Nagumo turned his carriers into the wind and sped up to twenty-four knots to give lift to his planes.

* * *

The Honolulu Star–Bulletin front–paged for its Saturday edition, December 6 a story fittingly illustrated by an Army sentry standing by an American flag. The caption read: "Army on the alert."

Lieutenant Commander Edwin T. Layton, intelligence officer for the Pacific Fleet, was worried. The radio eavesdroppers who monitored Japan's naval signals to try and track warship movements hadn't been able to pinpoint the location of their carriers. This was not unprecedented. The Navy had "lost" the carriers twelve times in the last six months. Usually this was because they were in home port in contact by land telephone lines instead of radio. Nonetheless, coupled with much radio "noise" and intercepted codes that indicated Japan's fleet was moving south, the carriers' absence from the picture was bothersome. Layton had prepared a report on the carriers for Kimmel a few days before. He had to confess he could only assume they were in home waters but couldn't be sure.

"What!" the admiral exploded. "You don't know where Carrier Division 1 and Carrier Division 2 are?"

"No, sir, I do not. I think they are in home waters, but I do not know ... The rest of these units, I feel pretty confident of their locations."

Halfway between jest and cold eye from the bridge, Kimmel said: "Do you mean to say that they could be rounding Diamond Head and you wouldn't know it?"

"I hope they would be sighted before now," said the abashed intelligence officer.

On that last Saturday of peace, Layton took Winant's warning of the Malaya–bound Japanese armada over to Vice Admiral William Pye on Battleship Row. Pye asked his opinion on the significance. Layton said the question was whether the Japanese would take the Philippines on their way south.

"Do you think they will leave their flank open?" asked the admiral.

"They never have," Layton replied.

"They will never go to war with the United States," said the admiral. "We're too big, too powerful. Too strong." He turned to his chief of staff, Captain Harold C. Train. "Harold, do you agree?"

"Emphatically."

Pearl had received its war warning a week ago, but this did not mean peacetime life did not go on under the aloha trade wind skies. That afternoon, locals cheered on the University of Hawaii as they took visiting gridders from stateside Williamette University, 20–6.

Uncle Sam's two carriers in the Pacific (the third, Saratoga, was in a yard on the West Coast under repair) were playing a deadlier game. Lexington was delivering planes to Midway Island to beef up its defense. Enterprise, Admiral William "Bull" Halsey commanding, was doing the same for the garrison at Wake Island. Lexington, in fact, had been spotted by Japanese sub I–74 which began tracking her. The sub could not fire torpedoes, however. Orders were to lay low until 8 a.m., Sunday, December 7 Hawaiian time. No explanation was given.

Halsey assumed the worst and ordered his Task Force 8 to operate under war

Vice Admiral William F. Halsey peering from the bridge of his ship somewhere in the Pacific.

conditions. Any Japanese shipping was to be sunk, any of their planes shot down. His operations officer, Commander William A. Buracker, protested.

"Goddamit, admiral, you can't start a private war of your own. Who's going to take the responsibility?"

"I'll take it," said Halsey. "If anything gets in my way, we'll shoot first and argue afterward."

Maneuvering, however, had cost Enterprise time. It was going to be late for its scheduled Sunday morning docking at Pearl. The crew moaned at losing half a weekend liberty. They took consolation in watching Gary Cooper play Sergeant

Secretary of the Navy Frank Knox reported on December 15 that the U.S. battleship Arizona and five other warships were lost in the Japanese air raid on Pearl Harbor naval base.

A Japanese carrier in north Pacific preparing to attack Pearl Harbor on December 7, 1941.

York on the ship's movie screen. There would be no carriers in port that Sunday morning at Pearl Harbor.

Some twenty-three hundred miles away Major General H.H. "Hap" Arnold, head of the Army Air Corps, had traveled to Hamilton Field near Sacramento to personally see off a flight of thirteen B–17s destined for MacArthur in the Philippines by way of Hawaii. The first leg to Hickam Field took fourteen hours, so the big bombers flew with only four–man crews and were unarmed. One of the pilots objected. At least they ought to carry their bomb sights and machine guns. Arnold said they could be put aboard but without ammunition to save weight.

So the bombers could home in on its signal, Major General Frederick L. Martin, head of the Hawaiian Air Force, had his staff ask station WGMB in Honolulu to stay on all night. Sure thing, general. Another night of ukuleles and Glenn Miller drifting out across the Pacific courtesy of the U.S. Army Air Corps.

When Lieutenant Colonel George W. Bicknell of Army intelligence heard about it, he blew up. Why tip our hands whenever we have planes coming in? Why not keep WGMB on the air every night?

One of those who caught the station was Lieutenant Kermit Tyler on his way to work the graveyard shift at the radar coordinating station at Fort Shafter. Must be planes coming in from the States, he told himself.

Washington was tense that Saturday. Code breakers had already read thirteen parts of a fourteen–part message from Tokyo to its negotiators in Washington, Kichisaburo Nomura and Saburo Kurusu. Nomura was a former admiral who had been summoned from retirement in 1940 to be ambassador to Washington. He was an unlikely choice. He was well disposed to the Americans, who admired his sincerity and could also look them in the eye, being six feet tall, immense for a Japanese. He walked with a limp, having been wounded by a terrorist in Shanghai in 1932. Nomura had low expectations that he could bring peace between his homeland and a nation he admired. After the war he told Gordon W. Prange, perhaps the definitive chronicler of Pearl Harbor: "When a big house falls, one pillar cannot stop it."

The Japanese ambassador to the United States, Kichisaburo Nomura (right), and special Japanese envoy to the United States, Saburo Kurusu, shown as they waited to see Secretary of State Cordell Hull, December 5, 1941.

Japan's Yoshikawa Mitsusada, Admiral Kichisaburo Nomura, Saburo Kurusu, and Captain Mitsuo Fuchida (left to right) were cogs in the Japanese machine that attacked Pearl Harbor. Mitsusada directed Tokyo's FBI counterpart. Nomura, ambassador to the United States, and Kurusu conducted peace talks in Washington right up to the time of the attack. Fuchida led the Japanese carrier plane forces that hit Pearl Harbor.

This Saturday his embassy was doing its best. A reduced staff was hung over from a farewell party given departing colleagues. Because stenographers were not allowed to read top–secret messages, embassy staffer Katsuzo Okamura was drafted to type out the fourteen–part message. And he was not the best typist in the world. In fact, the code breakers had read copies of the text before the Japanese embassy did.

The text said that the fourteenth and last part of the message would be transmitted later. Sometime after 9 p.m. Lieutenant Commander Alwin D. Kramer of the Navy's translation section delivered the pouch with the first thirteen parts to the White House.

The president's wife, Eleanor, was hosting a party but Roosevelt preferred the seclusion of his White House study and the company of his chief aide, Harry Hopkins. Roosevelt read the message, then turned to Hopkins: "This means war."

"Since war is undoubtedly going to come at the convenience of the Japanese, it's too bad we can't strike the first blow," Hopkins mused.

"No, we can't do that," Roosevelt cautioned. "We are a democracy and a peaceful people. But we have a good record."

Roosevelt was about to pick up the phone and inform Chief of Naval Operations Admiral Harold R. Stark, but thought better of it. Stark was attending a performance of "The Student Prince" and Roosevelt didn't want to upset the audience by publicly paging the Navy's commander.

Roosevelt had other things on his mind as well. He had just sent a last–minute message to Emperor Hirohito hoping the two leaders could head off war. "... Both of us ... have a sacred duty to restore traditional amity and prevent further death and destruction in the world," the president had written.

* * * * *

It was a quiet evening of uneasiness in the nation's capital. General George C. Marshall, commander in chief of the Army, spent a peaceful evening at home with his wife. Stimson had decided to spend the weekend at his Washington estate, Woolsey, overlooking Branch Brook, rather than go home to his Long Island one. "The atmosphere indicated something was going to happen," he wrote in his diary.

Colonel William J. "Wild Bill" Donovan, head of the new Office of Coordination of Information, which would become the Office of Strategic Service which would become the Central Intelligence Agency, was guest at a dinner party at the home of Ferdinand Lamont Berlin, former ambassador to Poland. But Donovan had a date next afternoon in New York. He was going to the Polo Grounds to watch the football Giants play the Brooklyn Dodgers. It was Tuffy Leemans Day. Alphonse Leemans had come out of George Washington University to star at fullback for six years with the Giants. The Dodgers were scarcely defenseless. They had their own fullback star in Pug Manders from Drake and halfback Ace Parker out of Duke. National League Football wasn't what it was to become, but 55,051 fans filled the Polo Grounds for Tuffy. In Washington, a young Bostonian, John F. Kennedy, planned to watch the Redskins.

There was another meeting that Saturday in Washington, seemingly as remote from December 6 as the next century. Dr. Vannevar Bush, late of MIT, chaired a sit–down of the brand new Office of Scientific Research and Development in the many–pillared Executive Office Building next door to the White House. One of its members, James Conant, young president of Harvard, summarized the meeting's decision: "The possibility of atomic bombs is great enough to justify an all-out effort." This was to be passed across the lawn to the White House "in" basket to wait its turn amid more urgent business.

* * * * *

28

NEW YORK GIANTS
vs.
BROOKLYN DODGERS

LEEMANS' DAY

TUFFY LEEMANS

**POLO
GROUNDS**

**Sunday
December 7, 1941**

In Hawaii, five-and-a-half hours behind Washington time, Saturday night was Saturday night. Sailors turned out for "The Battle of Music" between bands from battleship Row at the new recreation center named for Rear Admiral Claude C. Bloch, commanding officer of the Hawaii naval district. The bands took turns on "I Don't Want to Set the World on Fire" and "Take the A-Train." The ensemble from the battleship Pennsylvania won, but many thought Arizona's second–place band was better. The winners' reward was to sleep in Sunday.

Less musically inclined servicemen spilled out into honky–tonks — Two Jacks Bar, The Anchor. But the MPs were pleased to report only twenty-five unruly drunks among the island's 42,952–man garrison.

Ruth Flynn, secretary to the head of the FBI in Honolulu, Robert Shivers, had zombies and dinner with a date she could care less about. She got home early and started receiving calls every five minutes from Lieutenant Bucky Walsh of battleship Arizona. He urged her to turn out for the monthly wedding anniversary of shipmate Lieutenant Jim Dare and his wife, Jinny. She gave in and was glad she did. It was one of the best anniversary parties yet. So good, in fact, that Walsh stayed over that night with the Dares. "That's why he's alive today," Ruth said much later.

Another Arizonan, Ensign Everett Malcolm, got his fiancee home at 2 a.m. Sunday morning. Instead of heading back to the ship, he bunked in at the oft–frequented bachelor digs of Captain D.C. Emerson, who'd been dentist on the battleship.

General Short attended a popular dinner dance put on for charity by Ann Etzler, one of the talented members of the Army family, at Schofield Barracks. He and his wife packed it in at 10:30 p.m. He had a golf date the next morning with Kimmel. He drove home by way of the harbor. The lights of Battleship Row spangled the waters like a dance floor. "What a target that would make," said the general.

Kimmel himself had his usual single drink at a small gathering at the Halekulani Hotel with the Pyes and Rear Admiral Milo F. Draemel, skipper of cruiser Detroit. Kimmel told Draemel that Nagao Kita, the Japanese consul in Honolulu, had asked him to drop by for champagne at a stag party he frequently gave.

"Don't go," said Draemel, who sensed the way the wind was blowing.

"Don't worry, I won't," said Kimmel.

Nightly blackouts in Honolulu didn't interfere with service in this restaurant, which installed a "blackout door."

Draemel headed back to spend the night on his ship just in case something happened. Kimmel was in bed by 10 o'clock.

Layton danced at the Royal Hawaiian Hotel until the band closed up at midnight with "The Star Spangled Banner."

Despite the lateness of the hour — Tokyo was ten hours ahead and across the International Date Line from Washington — Ambassador Grew finally got Roosevelt's message to Hirohito. It had been intentionally delayed by the Japanese army. Grew roused Lord Privy Seal Marquis Koichi Kido who said he would try and contact the emperor even though it was 3 a.m.

At Pearl Harbor, workmen banged away well into the night at Drydock 1 where destroyers Cassin and Downes and battleship Pennsylvania were under repair. Ed Sheehan, an iron worker, stopped by to chat with Downes' duty bos'n who was addressing Christmas cards. Sheehan, a stateside native, had been in the islands long enough to pick up some lingo. "Know how to say 'Merry Christmas' in Hawaiian?" he offered. "Mele Kalikimake."

Not everybody else in Hawaii was sleeping in or sleeping it off. Privates Joseph L. Lockard and George E. Eliott had 4 a.m. duty to touch off the radar at Kahuku Point. Eliott had only worked the set for two weeks and wanted to practice on this wonder that could see one hundred and thirty miles out to sea.

Three U.S. warships were on patrol at the entrance to Pearl Harbor, minesweepers Condor and Crossbill sweeping to and fro and destroyer Ward. Antares, a supply ship with a lighter in tow, was coming in from Palmyra Island to deliver the barge to a tug for delivery into Pearl. Up above, Ensign William Tanner scanned the moonlight–flecked waters from his patrolling PBY. He had standing orders to depth–charge any submarines sighted in forbidden areas.

Ward was under the command of Lieutenant William Outerbridge, born of a British merchant captain and an Ohio girl in Hong Kong. He grew up in the States and graduated from Annapolis in 1927. Ward was his first command on his very first patrol as skipper. He was the only Naval Academy man on board. The rest of his officers were reservists from Minnesota, of all places, whose only prior sea duty had been Lake Superior.

It was still dark when Mrs. William Blackmore drove her husband through the Pearl Harbor gates. Blackmore was chief engineer of the tug Keosanqua that was heading out to rendezvous with Antares and relieve it of its burden. Mrs. Blackmore looked around the sleeping naval base.

"This is the quietest place I've ever seen," she said.

2
THE
RAPID DEATH
OF SAKOKU

An old painting shows the landing of Commodore Perry at Uraga on the shores of Tokyo Bay in 1853.

33

The road to Pearl Harbor properly begins with another fleet, in another time ...

This time there would be no *kamikaze* — the Divine Wind.

Indeed, these four dark ships defied the wind of Edo Bay to the utter amazement of throngs of Japanese gathered on shore. They traveled directly into it, leaving plumes of black smoke astern. Thus commenced the visit of Commodore Matthew Calbraith Perry to Japan in 1853, an epochal voyage that was to be disastrously reversed eighty–eight years later at Pearl Harbor.

Perry's American squadron, bearing a letter from President Millard Fillmore, was as baffling to the Japanese as they were to Perry. To whatever extent the Japanese then and later were to be judged enigmatic and idiosyncratic lies in a basic geographical fact. Japan is an island nation. For better or worse, it lies cast in the sea, isolated. Isolation may foster through lack of contacts a fear and mistrust of foreigners, even paranoia. And. lacking evidence to the contrary, it can nurture a feeling of superiority over mysterious other mortals beyond the horizon.

Writes Edwin O. Reischauer, former U.S. ambassador to Tokyo and a leading scholar of the Japanese: "Japanese ... view the rest of the world, including even their close cultural and racial relatives in Korea and China, with an especially strong 'we' and 'they' dichotomy...Isolation then permitted the Japanese to hold on to outmoded forms and institutions even when reality had passed them by."

His iron ships attested that Perry came from a world well into the Industrial Age. The land he viewed from his quarterdeck was through the looking glass, a feudal society scarcely changed through many centuries. The odd–appearing people he saw on shore believed their emperor was a human descendant of the sun goddess and that they and their islands were of divine origin. The view from those islands, showing nothing but ocean to the contrary, offered little to rebut that belief.

A Japanese print showing Commodore Perry and his men on the streets of Yokohama in 1854 (shown in the Library of Congress exhibition of American Battle Art, 1944).

Hirata Atsutane, born the same year Americans half a world away were declaring the equality of mankind in their Declaration of Independence, was to say as a leader among his people: "The Japanese ... are superior to all other countries of the world."

That no one rose to contradict him is not surprising. The only non–Japanese on the island were a few Dutch traders on the small island of Deshima off Nagasaki. None of their books, particularly Bibles, were to be taken ashore. Periodically the Dutch, virtual prisoners, were taken to Edo, now Tokyo, and forced to crawl on their bellies before the *shogun,* then play drunk and dance to amuse him. To prove they were not contaminated by their "barbaric" Christian religion, they were compelled to stomp on a cross.

Feudal Japan was a militaristic culture. The emperor was a figurehead. The real power lay with the *shogun,* his generalissimo since 1192, when the emperor handed temporal power to Minamoto Yonitoto, his most powerful general. The *shogun* tried to keep his head, often literally, amidst the competing two hundred and fifty or so land–holding lords, the *daimyo.* Serving them as mercenaries were the next highest caste in the pecking order, the *samurai.* These men of glowering mien, leather armor and wondrously sharp swords represented a national ideal: warriors of unalloyed loyalty, bravery and integrity. The Japanese esteem for these

Ancient Japanese warrior.

soldierly virtues abided long after Commodore Perry had sailed away. He should well have noted two other elements of the samurai code, *bushido*. One:

Win first, fight later.

Another:

Once the samurai's sword has been withdrawn, even to the thickness of a tea leaf, it must not be reinserted into its scabbard until it has drawn the blood of an enemy.

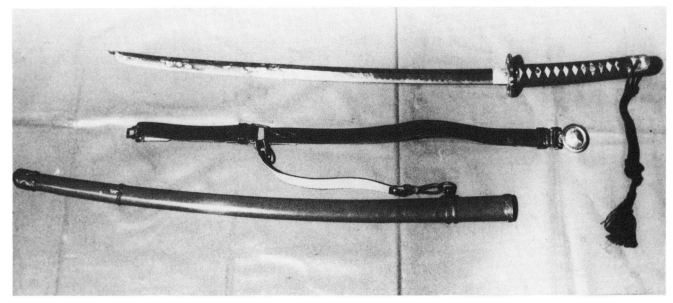

A samurai sword, belt and sheath.

While the Japanese believed their descent was from Jinmu, the first human emperor and fifth in line of descent from the sun goddess, their laws, government and pictograph writing, and much else, had Chinese origins. Notwithstanding, the Japanese on their islands were often fiercely xenophobic. Never had an alien conqueror trod their soil. In August 1281, Kublai Khan had put to sea with his Mongol army to invade Japan. A typhoon — the god–inspired Divine Wind — shattered the fleet.

In 1543, the Portuguese were allowed to establish a tiny trading post offshore of Kyushu. The missionary, St. Francis Xavier, visited from 1549 to 1551. By 1580 there were one hundred and fifty thousand Christians in Japan. But early in the next century, the Tokugawa family took over the shogunate. Japan became *sakoku,* the closed country. Christians were massacred. No foreigner was allowed to enter the country. Any fisherman or voyager who ventured overseas was not allowed to return on pain of death lest he contaminate with "forbidden thoughts." Japanese coastal vessels were forbidden to communicate with foreign craft. Thus, construction of ocean–going boats was banned. Japan closed the curtain on itself from the world for two hundred and fifty years, aside from the Dutch at Nagasaki and a few Chinese middlemen in Okinawa. In the late 18th century, a few enterprising American captains tried unsuccessfully to trade with Japan, their ships disguised as Dutch. After 1807, no American even tried.

But beyond the seas the world was changing.

In 1844, after the Opium War with China, Great Britain forced the Chinese to cede them Hong Kong and open five ports to trading. The United States also won rights to five ports. Imperialism was reaching into Asia. Directly affecting this was the American acquisition in the 1840s of California from Mexico via war and the Oregon Territory from Britain via treaty. The United States now had a window on the Pacific. Commerce beckoned. Japan was something of an invisible black hole in the way.

In 1837 an Anglo–American firm tried to repatriate seven Japanese shipwrecked sailors who had landed at the mouth of the Columbia River. Its vessel was fired on by the Japanese. In 1846 U.S. Commodore James Biddle, on the sloop–of–war Vincennes, arrived in Edo Bay, tried a chummy approach to present a letter from Washington. He was unceremoniously pushed, in full uniform, back into his longboat. After the Mexican War, Commodore James Glynn defied armed Japanese at Nagasaki to repatriate fifteen shipwrecked American sailors who reported of harsh treatment by the Japanese.

There were a few slits in the silk curtain, however. A few Japanese had been reading contraband Western books smuggled by the Dutch traders, euphemistically defined as "scholars." In 1843 a teen–aged Japanese castaway named Nakahama Manjiro was rescued by an American whaler. He attended school in Fair Haven, Massachusetts, took off for California with the '49 Gold Rush and eventually made it home to Japan. Instead of losing his head, he was interrogated at great length. Manjiro told his inquisitors that the United States had no territorial ambitions in Asia. He detailed the Mexican War to his amazed audience who were further startled to hear that Americans were inclined to read while sitting on the john. Instead of execution, Manjiro was made a samurai. Most of his countrymen continued to call foreigners "outer barbarians" and think them nothing more than "hairy pirates."

But increasingly, U.S. whalers and steamships were plying the Pacific.

In 1851 Captain J.A. Aulick of the U.S. Navy was chosen to go to Edo to

38

Painting made in 1883 showing the first electric light erected on Ginza street. Coach in center is horse-drawn railway, the most modern mass transportation means of the time.

extract a treaty for repatriation of shipwrecked Americans and to permit U.S. steamships to buy coal in Japan. Speaking like a true colonialist, golden–tongued Daniel Webster said coal was "a gift of Providence deposited by the great Creator of all things in the depths of the Japanese islands for the benefit of the human family." Aulick was not to collect on Providence's gift, falling victim to ill health and gossip — false — that he had nepotistically given his son a free trip to Asia and tried to shake down a Brazilian diplomat. Perry, brother of the victor of the Battle of Lake Erie and his immortal signal: "We have met the enemy and they are ours," was a gruff, jowly old salt who was given the touchy job of opening Japan.

His fleet contained something of a time capsule of all the centuries the Japanese had missed. He took along an Italian bandmaster, a French chef, two folios of Audubon prints of American birds, champagne, some new revolvers invented by Samuel Colt, mirrors, farm tools, clocks, a daguerrotype camera, a telegraph recently invented by Samuel Morse, and a one–quarter–scale steam locomotive. And some French perfume for the ladies. The crew was hand–picked for youth. Grizzled sea dogs were deemed to be unruly and too set in their dissolute waterfront ways. This was to be an errand of diplomatic finesse, as President Fillmore made explicit in his orders:

" ... If after having exhausted every argument, he [Perry] will then change his tone and inform them [the Japanese] ... that if any sets of cruelty should hereafter

Shanghai in 1932, looking west on the Whangpo River from the Bund Bridge.

be practiced on the citizens of his country, whether by the government or inhabitants of Japan, they will be severely chastized."

Perry, bandmaster, chef, et al, dropped anchor in Edo Bay July 8, 1853, to instant consternation ashore. Twenty thousand samurai were immediately summoned. The price of armor quadrupled. With the help of the Dutch, Japanese guard boats sailed up with a sign in French: "Depart immediately and dare not anchor."

Perry insisted on presenting Fillmore's letter personally and ceremoniously. Ultimately, he prevailed. He was astonished to get a reply in English. It had been written by Nakahama Manjiro, the ex–Massachusetts high schooler.

(The U.S. ensign Perry flew on the day of the presentation was to fly from the quarterdeck of the battleship Missouri in Tokyo Bay ninety–two years later at another American–Japanese ceremony.)

Perry came ashore with great pomp and was received accordingly. He did not know it, but ten samurai lurked under the reception floor ready to kill him in the event of American treachery. Instead, Perry was beleaguered by Japanese asking him to autograph their fans. He was given one hundred specimens for his shell collection. American sailors ogled and prodded the biceps of sumo wrestlers who helped re–supply the American fleet, carrying aboard two one–hundred–pound bags of rice at a time. Meanwhile, samurai delightedly rode around and around atop the tiny train, their brocaded robes streaming behind at twenty miles an hour.

Perry returned a year later to sign a formal treaty. Article I referred to "perfect, permanent and universal peace and a sincere, cordial amity" between the two nations. Actually, the Japanese thought the Americans, notwithstanding their French chef, had boorish table manners. They couldn't use chopsticks and talked loudly during meals. But rarely, if ever, has a nation transformed itself so rapidly and dramatically as Japan did in going from sakoku to the Western industrial age almost overnight.

Sakoku was killed in the first act. By the 1860s, the rule of the emperor as custodian of Japan's holy soil and soul conflicted increasingly with the temporal power of the shogun, who had to deal with the hated foreigners of the post–Perry period. A slogan took root: *Sonno Joi* –– "Honor the emperor, expel the barbarians." In 1867 the old emperor died, to be succeeded by his fifteen–year–old son, Mutsushito. He, as all emperors, was to take a name he chose to characterize his reign. His was *Meiji* — Enlightened Government.

In short order, after a failed rebellion, the shogunate was abolished and daimyo and samurai lost their feudal privileges. Japan quickly began building a modern military under a new slogan: *Fukoku, keyohei* — "Rich country, strong army."

The reasons were twofold. Only a modern army and navy, the Japanese reasoned, could keep them from being subverted and carved up like China by Western imperialism. Also, awakening Japan, suddenly realizing it had neighbors, perceived them from its warlike tradition. Within fifty years it was to war with all of them: Korea, China, and, finally, Russia. The sleeping samurai did not come in peace once awakened. Japan was victorious in each instance. This can be attributed to the same geographical accident that prompted Japan's paranoic xenophobia. An island people.

Isolation on their islands left the Japanese a homogenous race, one that could respond swiftly and with unanimity once challenged. The Meiji governments inherited an efficient bureaucracy and high literacy. Things could get done. A conscript army was promptly raised, modeled after Prussia's. Peasants, once at the low end of the socio–economic scale (except for the Eta and Hubub classes who were held to be "not human"), now proudly were Japan's two hundred and seventy five thousand–man army, inheritors of samurai tradition they previously were denied.

Their first target was Korea, a barbarous backwater known as "the Hermit Kingdom." To the Japanese, Korea was "an arrow pointed at the heart of Japan" if occupied by a foreign power. China had dominant foreign influence over the fragmented Korean kingdom which the Japanese successfully challenged in the Sino–Japanese War of 1895. By the Treaty of Shimonoseki, China ceded Japan Formosa, the Kwantung Peninsula guarding the sea approaches to Peking, and gave Japan a "most favored" position in China itself.

Suddenly awakened themselves to a new boy on the block, Russia, Germany and France pressured Japan to give up the peninsula. Russia was given instead a twenty–five year lease by the Chinese on Port Arthur at the tip of it. Japan was not strong enough to object but quietly seethed with resentment. It quadrupled its military budget.

Japan helped the Western nations quell the Boxer rebellion in China in 1900 and in 1903 agreed with Russia that its interests were paramount in Manchuria while Japan's would be in Korea. But Japan was beginning to feel hemmed in. Russia had built the Trans–Siberian railroad all the way to the Pacific at Vladivostok. The United States had taken over the Philippines. Manchuria, its coal and grain coveted in a resource–poor Japan, beckoned.

By 1904, Japanese negotiators were in St. Petersburg trying to reach an accord.

Illustration from a photo of the Japanese battleship Mikasa fighting against a Russian squadron off Port Arthur during the Russo-Japanese War on August 10, 1904.

Russian soldiers hauling guns up the steep heights of Port Arthur.

The ensuing parallels to Pearl Harbor are striking. The czar told his military that Japan should fire the first shot should it come to war. Roosevelt said the same. The Russian viceroy on the Kwantung peninsula told the naval commandant, an Admiral Stark — same name as the U.S. naval commander in 1941 — that war preparedness would be "premature." The American Stark received similar advice years later.

And, most significantly, the Japanese struck first, declared war later. On February 4, 1904, the Japanese broke off negotiations in St. Petersburg. Two days later a Japanese fleet slipped out of Sasebo bound for Port Arthur. Near midnight on the 8th, a Monday, the Japanese attacked the Russian fleet while it was coaling with most of its men ashore — presumably drinking and philandering in the expected Western fashion. Two Russian battleships were crippled and a cruiser and gunboat destroyed.

Two days later Japan declared war. Both Port Arthur and Mukden, the Manchurian capital, were besieged and eventually captured. In May 1905, Russia's European fleet, having raced around the Cape of Good Hope to Asia, lost thirty–four of its thirty–seven ships to the Japanese at the battle of Tsushima Straits, one of history's most one–sided sea fights. Some four thousand eight hundred and thirty Russian sailors drowned. Japan lost three torpedo boats and one hundred and ten men.

Two points to remember: the victorious admiral was Heihachiro Togo, whose final flag signal to the fleet read: "The Empire's fate depends on the result of this battle. Let every man do his utmost duty." It was a message that would bear repeating. Also: a young Japanese ensign lost two fingers of his left hand at Tsushima. His name was Isoroku Yamamoto. His father had been a samurai. The fruits of surprise had not been lost on either of them.

Acting as a peacemaker, President Theodore Roosevelt invited both combatants to a parlay in Portsmouth, New Hampshire, that September. The advocate of speaking softly and carrying a big stick was to extract the following settlement for which he received a Nobel peace prize:

— Russia accepted Japan's "paramount" interest in Korea.

— It ceded its Port Arthur lease to the Japanese plus the South Manchurian Railway and half of Sakhalin Island. Japan was allowed to station troops along the railroad and engage in business in Manchuria. But both sides were to evacuate their troops from there.

The Japanese also wanted a cash indemnity. Roosevelt balked at this. He thought it would make Japan too powerful. This persuaded some officers of the Imperial Navy that the West could not be trusted. Increasingly, naval strategy turned towards the one neighboring power Japan had not yet fought, now perceived by some as the ultimate enemy. The United States of America.

******

In just a half–century, the Meiji period had left Japan a major player on the world stage. In 1905, Japan had muscled Korea into its protectorate. Five years later, the Hermit Kingdom was annexed outright. Japan had become a colonial power. But it did so under a new slogan: Asia for Asians.

The Empire, however, had entered late in the game, at a time of growing

Emperor Hirohito on his favorite white mount, inspecting the Imperial Armed Forces troops during a military review at the Yoyogi drill field in Tokyo, October 21, 1940. (Courtesy Kyodo News Service.)

nationalism, particularly in China. Asia for the Asians sounded suspiciously like Asia for the Japanese to some ears. However, the former island samurais, with celestial sanction, saw colonization as vital for a land of too few resources and too many people.

Yet twice in ten years the West had denied them what the Japanese perceived as the justified winnings of war. The reaction was that of an industrialized samurai. After Portsmouth, the Japanese began spending forty–three percent of their national budget on arms.

Matthew Perry had brought sakoku to a sudden end. If not he, assuredly someone else or some other nation would have. What the Meijis had replaced it with was uncertain. But the transformation was striking.

"I have today seen the most stupendous spectacle it is possible for the martial brain to conceive," said British General Sir Ian Hamilton of the Russo–Japanese fighting: "Asia advancing and Europe falling back."

A picture of Russian warships in the harbor at Port Arthur during the Russo-Japanese War. The Variag (second from right) was sunk during the battle with the Japanese fleet, and the Peresviet (extreme right) was disabled.

3
5:5:3
A RATIO

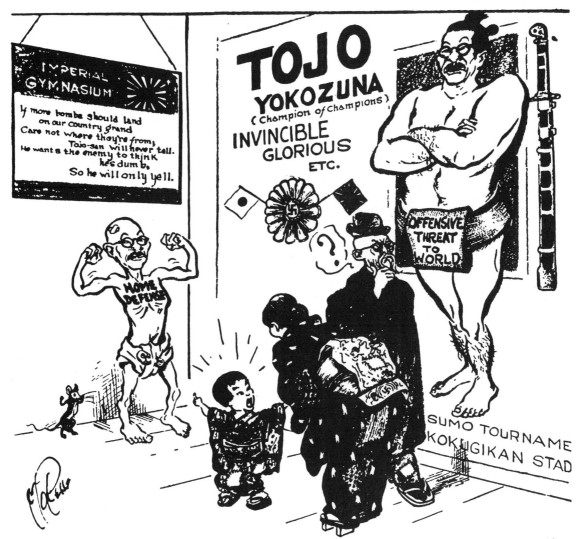

"Ooh, Mama-san! Grandpa-san! He Doesn't Look Anything Like His Picture!".

This cartoon was published in a Japanese language newspaper in Hawaii to give Japanese there an idea of the nature of the government in Japan. This one portrays the cartoonist's interpretation of Premier Tojo.

One of the most inscrutable Oriental traits to a Westerner is the concept of "face." Whatever the reality, appearances must be observed. As Japan took a seat at the world's table, as the Pacific shrunk, Japanese as individuals and as a nation ventured forth. The experience was not always happy.

By the turn of the century thousands of Japanese had migrated to the Hawaiian Islands and the West Coast of America. They came for opportunity, for new starts. By 1908 there were sixty thousand Japanese in California but they encountered the same racism earlier migrants from China had faced. American resentment focused on the willingness of Japanese immigrants to work for lower wages. West Coast labor organizations organized the Japanese and Korean Exclusion League. The idea of a "Yellow Peril" flood of Asians had resurfaced. In 1906 the San Francisco school board ordered all Orientals into a separate school. By a subsequent "Gentleman's Agreement," Japan agreed to curtail migration to the United States. But face had been lost for a proud and ancient people.

On another level, by the Root–Takahira Treaty of 1908, Japan and the United States agreed to support the status quo in the Pacific as well as the independence and "integrity" of China and maintaining the "Open Door" to international trade there. The Japanese interpreted the pact as de facto recognition of their predominant influence in Korea and Manchuria. Japanese expansionism took a more direct form with the outbreak of World War I. Japan, which had had a treaty with Great Britain since 1902, immediately seized Germany's concessions in China. Shortly after, Japanese forces took Germany's island possessions in the Pacific: Palau, the Marianas, the Carolines and the Marshalls. While Europe clawed at its vitals in the stalemated trenches of France, Japan in 1915 sought to strengthen itself on the Asian mainland with the humbling Twenty–One Demands upon China. These would have made China all but a Japanese protectorate and given the Empire a free hand in southern Manchuria even to Mongolia. China, beset by Sun Yat–sen's revolution, had no recourse but to submit.

50

Cryptographer Herbert O. Yardley.

William F. Friedman, leader of the task force that cracked the Japanese Purple code, posing at home in 1956.

The end of the world war, however, brought a change of climate. Colonialism and arms races were discredited as causes of the blood–letting. Perhaps the world could do better. A League of Nations was created as a forum for international peace efforts and a Naval Armament Conference convened in Washington in 1921.

Herbert O. Yardley was not there but he probably knew as much as any delegate in attendance. He eavesdropped.

Lady Luck pointed the way to Herbert Yardley, just as it often does when a sharp mind is noodling away in eye–glazing boredom in a cooped–up office. The same willy–nilly cross–current made William Frederick Friedman an even greater codebreaker, maybe the greatest ever.

* * * * *

President John Quincy Adams hired the country's first code clerk while he was Secretary of State 1817–1825. It remained a meager calling even when young Yardley signed on at age twenty–four for $17.50 a week as a clerk in 1913. America didn't have a hell of a lot to be secret about in those days and didn't pay much heed to any distant thunder in Europe. Yardley had been a so–so student growing up in Indiana, but he had a flair for math. Seventy years later he would have been a computer hacker. Back then he was a Morse code hacker. And, at State, bored. So bored he began cracking incoming code traffic. He'd found his muse. He deciphered a message to President Woodrow Wilson from Colonel Edward M. House, Wilson's top aide, in only two hours. Such talent got Yardley assigned to Army Intelligence when the United States entered the hush–hush world for real in 1917. He was appointed a lieutenant in cryptography.

The Army had another such lieutenant, William Frederick Friedman. Born near Odessa in 1891, he had been brought to America by his postal worker father to escape the pogroms sweeping through the Ukraine. Yardley eventually graduated from Cornell with a degree in his first love, genetics. He was settling into a post–graduate career of fruit flies and Mendelian imperatives at Cornell when a letter arrived. It was from Colonel (honorary) George Fabyan, a wealthy cotton broker and world class eccentric who was looking for a "would be-er, not an as-is-er" geneticist to help improve the flora and fauna on the farm at his Riverbank Laboratories outside Chicago.

George Fabyan had another passion: to prove that Sir Francis Bacon and not Shakespeare wrote Shakespeare. He had only to decipher the code he believed Sir

Francis had encrypted in "Troilus and Cressida" etc. and then bask ever after in the world's acclaim. His codebreaker was a similarly driven proper Bostonian, Elizabeth Wells Gallup. Mrs. Gallup's assistant was Elizebeth (her mother spelled it without an "a" so no one would call her Eliza) Smith.

When Friedman arrived at Riverbank in 1915, he brought with him an interest in photography. Mrs. Gallup asked him to take pictures of some Shakespeare folios. Friedman thereupon became fascinated with (a) Miss Smith and (b) cryptanalysis (a word he coined) and married both for life. "When it came to cryptology, something in me found an outlet," he was to say. "Just an inherent curiosity to know what people were trying to write that they didn't want other people to read."

While Sir Francis's hidden messages kept eluding Mrs. Gallup, the Army began sending cryptograms and coded messages to Riverbank. Friedman broke one, keyed from a book, without even knowing what the book was. When the war broke out, the Army signed Friedman up. After the war, Friedman, convinced Fabyan was a nut, nonetheless returned to Riverbank. The Army sent out a ciphered message it considered unbreakable. Friedman cracked it and sent back a letter to Washington in the same cipher. Convinced, the Army hired Friedman in 1921. One of the leading players of Pearl Harbor was now on stage. Or more accurately, backstage.

Yardley, meanwhile, had been set up in secret in midtown Manhattan with Army and State Department slush funds to run a codebreaking operation he called the Black Chamber. He began working on coded messages Tokyo was sending its delegation to the Washington Naval Conference. Publicly the Japanese were holding out for a 10:10:7 tonnage ratio in construction of capital ships with Britain, the United States and themselves respectively. Japan was by then spending almost half of its national budget on the military. But Yardley, who broke sixteen codes by the end of the conference, knew from intercepts that the Japanese would settle for 5:5:3. He advised U.S. negotiators to stand pat. They did. The Japanese gave in as predicted.

What the Japanese also didn't know, not having their own Yardley, was that since 1918 the U.S. Navy had made it its policy "to exercise in the Pacific a commanding superiority of naval power." The highly visible and increasing presence of American warships in the Pacific was evidence enough to make Tokyo uneasy.

The two English–speaking nations of the Pacific, New Zealand and Australia, wondered why this would make the Japanese apprehensive. Weren't they allies,

IDENTIFICATION OF JAPANESE FORCES

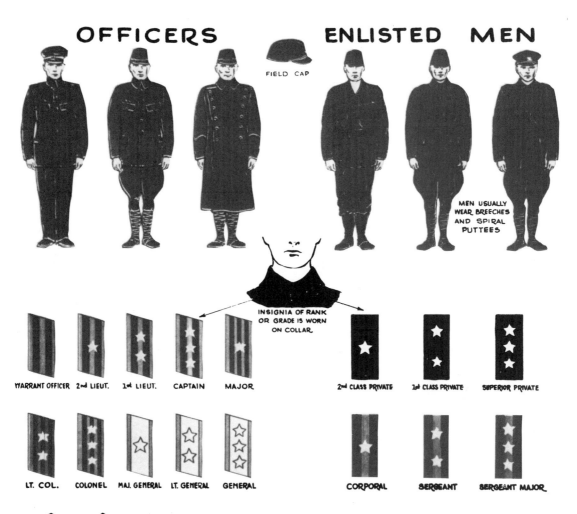

OFFICERS   FIELD CAP   **ENLISTED MEN**

MEN USUALLY WEAR BREECHES AND SPIRAL PUTTEES

INSIGNIA OF RANK OR GRADE IS WORN ON COLLAR.

WARRANT OFFICER   2nd LIEUT.   1st LIEUT.   CAPTAIN   MAJOR

2nd CLASS PRIVATE   1st CLASS PRIVATE   SUPERIOR PRIVATE

LT. COL.   COLONEL   MAJ. GENERAL   LT. GENERAL   GENERAL

CORPORAL   SERGEANT   SERGEANT MAJOR

ZIGZAG CHEVRON (LEFT) DENOTES BRANCH OF SERVICE. IT IS WORN ABOVE RIGHT SHIRT OR COAT POCKET.

RED-INFANTRY: YELLOW - ARTILLERY: GREEN- CAVALRY: MAROON - ENGINEERS: SKY BLUE - AVIATION: NAVY BLUE - BAND: BLUE-BLACK - TRANSPORT: DARK GREEN- MEDICAL: PURPLE-VETERINARY: BLACK - MILITARY POLICE.

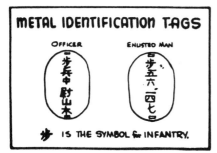

METAL IDENTIFICATION TAGS

OFFICER   ENLISTED MAN

步 IS THE SYMBOL for INFANTRY.

OTHER IDENTIFICATION:

SOMETIMES ENLISTED MEN CARRY A SMALL 'MILITARY NOTEBOOK' CONTAINING SOLDIER'S NAME, SERIAL NUMBER, AND MILITARY RECORD.

A copy of this poster once graced the bulletin boards in every post in the Hawaiian Islands. It shows types of uniforms and their collar tabs worn by soldiers in the Japanese armies.

after all? To them the U.S. fleet stood between them and the fate of Korea and the Pacific islands.

The Washington conference agreement was signed February 6, 1922. It limited capital ships to thirty-five thousand tons, carriers to twenty-seven thousand tons, guns to a maximum bore of sixteen inches. As if to show there were no hard feelings, the United States, Britain, France and Japan agreed to respect the status quo under the mandates of the League of Nations.

Behind the appearance of acceptance, however, some Japanese naval officers seethed. Yet again, Japan had lost face, relegated to a junior partnership. The Imperial Navy split into two. The "treaty faction" composed of admirals trained by the British respected a treaty as being a treaty. The anti–treaty group were motivated "by romantic idealism mixed with a plain old–fashioned desire for immense power," writes Stephen Howarth in "To Shining Sea: A History of the United States Navy." They claimed to embody the genuine spirit of Japan uncontaminated by foreign influence. It was a schism that was to widen as the waters of the Pacific narrowed.

* * * * *

One of the earliest and most fervent apostles of air power — he was later to be called a martyr — was Colonel William "Billy" Mitchell. He was found guilty of conduct prejudicial to military discipline in 1925 by a court–martial despite having bombed an old hulk to the bottom in a demonstration.

The lesson was not lost on the Imperial Navy. In 1922 the Japanese launched Hosho, the first carrier specifically built for aircraft. The United States had already converted a collier to an aircraft carrier and renamed it Langley. Two other ships, originally laid down as battle cruisers, were also converted and named Saratoga and Lexington. They weighed in at thirty–three thousand tons, above the Washington Treaty limits. The United States lamely said the extra weight was "for providing means against air and submarine attack." The explanation did not convince the "fleet faction" in Tokyo.

That group did not include the Japanese naval attache in Washington at the time of the Mitchell affair, the man with two fingers missing from his left hand. He had been too impressed by America's industrial power to think his nation could or should challenge it. But Isoroku Yamamoto was equally impressed by Billy Mitchell's demonstration of what bombs could do to a targeted warship, even a hulk.

When Captain James Cook discovered the Hawaiian Islands in 1778, Pearl Harbor was called "Wai Momi," meaning "water of pearl," taking its name from the pearl oysters that thrived in its waters.

Americans being evacuated from Nanking heading for the Panay to escape hostilities on December 11, 1937. This was the last departure of the Panay, which had stood by for weeks to safeguard Americans.

Pearl Harbor then was unsuitable as a port site because a dead coral reef blocked its entrance to all but shallow draft vessels. It remained undeveloped until the late 19th century, when several nations sought to obtain it as a fuel and supply base.

In 1840, U.S. Navy Lieutenant Charlie Wilkes led a geodetic expedition to the South Seas, stopping in Hawaii. He surveyed the Pearl Harbor estuary and reported that "if the water upon the bar should be deepened, which I doubt not can be effected, it would afford the best and most capacious harbor in the Pacific." Six years later an English sea captain made a British bid for the inlet, sending word back to Queen Victoria that all the ships in the world could fit into Pearl River, as it was then called.

In 1873, Major General J.M. Schofield and Lieutenant Colonel B.S. Alexander were sent to Honolulu to inspect the defensive capacity of Oahu. They reported that "Pearl River is a fine sheet of deep water extending inland about six miles from its mouth, the depth of water after passing the bar is ample for any vessel." A long period of negotiations followed with the Hawaiian monarchy, ending with the United States obtaining exclusive rights to Pearl Harbor in 1884. In exchange, Congress agreed to allow Hawaiian sugar to enter the United States duty free.

Clearing the coral bar across the harbor entrance was delayed for nearly two decades until the Spanish-American War confirmed the strategic value of Pearl Harbor as an advance naval base. It was not until 1900 that dredging of the entrance was begun.

In 1908, the Appropriation Act of 13 May declared that "the Secretary of the Navy is hereby authorized and directed to establish a naval station at Pearl Harbor, Hawaii, on the site heretofore acquired for that purpose and to erect thereat all the necessary machine shops, storehouses, coal sheds, and other necessary buildings."

The 14th Naval District, with headquarters at Pearl Harbor, was established in 1916, and three years later a $27 million construction program was launched.

Activity at Pearl Harbor reached an all-time peak during World War II, when the civilian force at the naval shipyard climbed to 26,000 employees.

Today, Pearl Harbor is a busy city in itself, with more than seventy naval commands and a network of shops, churches, clubs, restaurants, recreational facilities and offices.

4
THE REIGN OF SHOWA

Japanese soldiers attacking Chinese in Manchuria in 1936.

In the 1930s, Japan became a samurai to the world.

In a series of stage-managed outbreaks of belligerence that were euphemistically called "incidents," the Japanese partially drew the sword of war from its scabbard. Increasingly, parallels were to be drawn with the Empire of the Rising Sun and the Third Reich of Adolf Hitler half a globe away. Using to their fullest the emotional and dramatic tools of propaganda, Hitler preached to the Germans who had been a nation only since 1870 that they were indeed a master race. The Japanese and their semi-divine emperor needed no such persuasion. Asia for Asians, Japanese Asians.

At home in Japan, murderous super-patriots reverted to what shocked onlookers called "government by assassination."

The Manchurian "Incident" was to be followed by the Shanghai "Incident," the China "Incident," the Panay "Incident," and then . . .

Manchuria had what mountainous, seagirt Japan had not. Large veins of coal. Steppes of grain rolling to the horizon. To Russians and Japanese, it had been where East met West. In 1928, it was semi-autonomous, the province of a Chinese warlord, Chang Tso-lin. But Japanese influence had predominated since the Russian war in 1905. Chang allowed Japanese advisers into his fiefdom. Resettled Japanese colonials tilled the fertile fields, supervised iron and coal mines. By the Treaty of Portsmouth, the Japanese were permitted to station troops along the South Manchurian Railroad connecting the Liaotung peninsula and its Kwantung province to the capital at Mukden and the Trans-Siberian Railroad. In fact, the Imperial troops, twenty thousand of them, were called the Kwantung Army. As it turned out, they, too, were semi-autonomous of Tokyo, insubordinately so.

Native Manchurians had driven off Japanese settlers. Chang was making overtures to Chiang Kai-shek, the new leader of China.

In 1927, Baron Tanaka met in Mukden for a conference. The result, the perhaps spurious Tanaka Memorial, was leaked. It detailed how Manchuria, Mongolia and then China were to be brought under Japanese influence. In particular, two Japanese colonels of the Kwantung Army, Seishiro Itagaki and Kanji Ishihara, were furrowing their brows as to how to cause an "incident" that would further Japan's domination. In 1928, Chang was killed in an explosion that dynamited his train. He was succeeded by his son, Chang Hsueh–liang. The problem persisted.

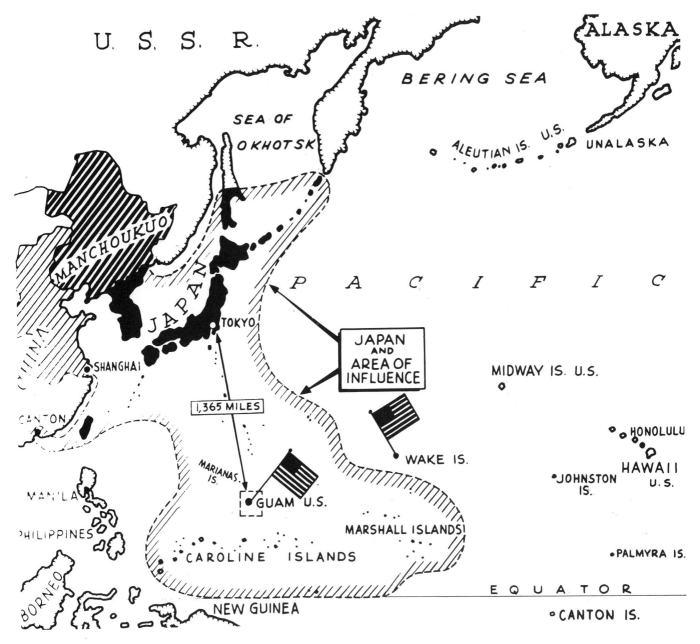

The newspaper Kokumin in Tokyo said editorially on January 16, 1939, that Japan would "smash the American fleet" if the United States intends to "get a political foothold in China" by fortifying Guam and Wake Island. As the map shows, Guam lies within the Japanese-dominated region.

Chang intrigued with Chiang and was prepared to let Chinese soldiers into Manchuria and allow the Chinese to build a competing railway to the South Manchurian. Somewhere in here the colonels of the Kwantung Army hid two 9.5–inch cannon in what ostensibly was a swimming pool across from the police station in Mukden. One was zeroed in on the station, the other the airfield. If history wouldn't oblige with a *causus belli,* it was time to hurry it along by manufacturing one.

Ishihara's dream was for an autonomous, multinational, socialized Manchuria, a home for Japan's excess population, a font of food and coal and a buffer against the Communist Soviet Union. His dream was shared with enough people back home that Japan was swept with "Manchuria Fever." The temperature rose appreciably when one Captain Shintero Nakamura was executed by some Chinese. Nakamura had been shot while on a trip to Inner Mongolia. He had been found to be carrying guns, a military map and narcotics, all suspicious in that nervous part of the world. Tokyo demanded a humiliating apology from China. Tokyo made a seeming show of conciliation by sending a general to Mukden, normally a day's train ride from the coast. The general, Yoshitsugu Tatekawa, thoughtfully gave the Kwantung colonels forty–eight hour advance notice of his arrival, thoughtful in that he was in on the plot.

Tatekawa had organized the assassination of the old warlord Chang Tso–lin and, for his extracurricular activities, was nicknamed The Fearless Pimp. He took three days to get to Mukden to give the plot time to hatch. Tatekawa finally made Mukden late on September 18, 1931. He was taken immediately to the Literary Chrysanthemum teahouse and provided with sake and a geisha girl. Colonel Itagaki couldn't party with the general because he just happened to be Mukden duty officer that night. At 10:20 p.m. Japanese secret police dynamited the Manchurian Railroad. (Actually about three feet of it; a train safely passed through shortly after the blast.)

At the sound of the explosion, Chinese troops had rushed out of the police station to see what was going on. There happened to be a patrol of Japanese soldiers right outside. Shots were exchanged. The cannon came out of the swimming pool and began firing away. A Japanese consular official who hadn't been tipped off tried to restore order. A Japanese officer threatened to run him through with his sword. Tatekawa allegedly was too drunk to lend his presence although he was seen later that night, sword in hand, leading a charge on the police station. The Japanese swiftly overran Mukden, then all of Manchuria.

Said General Sadao Araki: "Japan must no longer let the impudence of the white peoples go unpunished. It is the duty of Japan ... to cause China to expel foreign influence from Manchuria and to follow the way of imperial destiny."

62

New trouble broke out between Japan and Russia August 12, 1938, on Sakhalin Island, north of Japan, and increased tension between the two countries. At an isolated corner of the Russo-Japanese border (upper arrow), infantrymen of the NKVD, Soviet secret police, shot and wounded two Japanese policemen, according to Domei, the Japanese news agency. The incident occurred less than forty-eight hours after a truce at Changkufeng (lower arrow), on the mainland. Manchoukuo was the Japanese name given Manchuria.

Emperor Hirohito as a youth in navy uniform around 1921.

Manchuria became the Republic of Manchukuo — Land of the Manchus. Henry Pu Yi, the last emperor of China, was installed the following March as puppet ruler. By then there had been another incident, this one in Shanghai.

The Japanese community was the largest of the foreign concessions in that teeming city. It was protected by twenty–three warships and twenty–five hundred Marines. Outraged by the events in Manchuria, Shanghai Chinese began boycotting Japanese products. On January 18, 1932, some Japanese priests started a riot outside a Chinese factory which was later torched. The Japanese consul demanded of the mayor that he apologize and stop the boycott. The mayor said he was powerless to do so. On the 29th, the Japanese gave the Chinese half an hour to evacuate the Chapei section of the city. When time was up, Japanese carrier planes bombed the area with incendiaries. Thousands died. Two weeks later, Japanese troops attacked Chinese soldiers of the Nineteenth Route Army, notable for being one of the reliable units of Chiang Kai–shek.

A concerned United States sent the cruiser Houston, six destroyers and four hundred Marines to the city. Some leading Americans called for a boycott of Japan. Secretary of State Henry Stimson, using a discreet method to express the Hoover Administration's feeling, wrote Senator William E. Borah of Idaho a letter saying it had been U.S. policy since the Boxer Rebellion to maintain the integrity of China. The League of Nations appointed Lord Lytton of Great Britain to investigate the aggression. Japan replied it did not consider the Chinese an "organized people" as defined by the League for nationhood.

The Japanese had met their match in the Nineteenth Route Army and withdrew, but on December 7, 1932, a date that became infamous in Tokyo, the League adopted, 42–1, Lytton's report censuring Japan.

One of the Japanese delegates, Yosuke Matsuoka, told the League: "We are prepared to be crucified, but we do believe, and firmly believe that in a very few years world opinion will be changed, and that we also shall be understood by the world as Jesus of Nazareth was."

Three weeks later, the Kwantung Army occupied China's Jehol province just north of the Great Wall.

Tokyo assured Washington that Japan had no ambitions south of there. And on March 27, 1933, it said it was leaving the League which still had not learned to understand.

Admiral Montgomery Taylor, commander of the U.S. Asiatic Fleet, remarked grudgingly:

"One cannot help but admire the way the Japanese have been thumbing their nose at the rest of the world. The diplomatic corps of the nations seems to have gotten itself in something of a box with their high–sounding treaties which in this part of the world mean nothing."

* * * * *

There was no intended irony when the young Japanese emperor, Hirohito, chose a name for his reign. It was *showa,* which can be translated as "shining peace."

A retiring man whose loves were gardening and marine biology, he was the first emperor of Japan to have traveled to Europe, making a tour as crown prince. The early years of his reign encountered as much violence at home as they had abroad.

The political spectrum was divided between the Imperial Way (Kodo) faction and the Control (Tosei) faction. The former championed expansion into Manchuria, and a more aggressive handling of the Diet, the Japanese parliament. To them, the Soviets were enemy No. 1. To the Toseis, China was the foremost enemy. Both factions, more importantly, favored Japanese expansion.

On the far fringes there were others who looked for their guidance to Japan's feudal past. To them, politicians were corrupt (and many were) and businessmen selfish. Their ideal was the samurai: brave, loyal, selfless, indifferent to death. So were they. The samurai was also a man of violence, a killer. So were they.

They gathered in various bands. The Blood Brotherhood. The Love of Country Association. The Black Dragon. The Cherry Society. The Brocade Flag. They were super–patriotic and found a ready following in the military. They plotted and they assassinated. One plot by the Brocade Flag involved killing members of the Imperial court and government, then the assassins were to gather in front of the Royal Palace and commit hara–kiri in apology to the emperor.

By samurai tradition, assassination was not ignoble. In Japanese eyes, a man improvident enough to be assassinated showed a certain lack of virtue, particularly when the deed was committed by someone who claimed to be acting for the public good. By that reasoning, the murder of Prime Minister Yuko Namaguchi November 14, 1930, by a militant could be reasoned as deserved. His government had approved the result of the London Naval Conference earlier that year, which still did not bring Japan's fleet to parity with Britain and the United States. (Two years before, Japan had joined sixty–one nations in signing the Kellogg–Briand Treaty which "renounced war as an instrument of national policy." The London conference did up Japan's ratio to 10:10:7 for cruisers. The

General and Madame Chiang Kai-shek relax during a visit in Hunan province, which they visited after Chinese troops drove the Japanese from Changsha, the capital.

United States suspected the Japanese had already been building cruisers that were a third heavier than they admitted.)

Namaguchi's death set off a continuing series of political murders, avidly supported by young army firebrands of the Imperial Way faction. Each member of the Blood Brotherhood pledged to kill at least one business leader or corrupt politician. The reaction was peculiarly Japanese. One assassin was sentenced to twenty days — in a geisha house. Another was allowed to harangue the trial court at will against corruption and dirty politics.

"Government by assassination" reached the heights of something or other in 1932, when seventy–five–year–old Prime Minister Tsuyoshi Inukai invited the killers inside. Taking off their shoes, they did as he bid, came in and sat down. Then they shot their host.

Japanese grievances, real or imagined, flourished against this backdrop of political chaos and economic ruin. America had won its marks for sending the Navy with aid after an earthquake devastated Tokyo in 1923. The very next year, however, the Japanese were humiliated by U.S. immigration laws that excluded Asians. Japan had to trade to survive in a world it had only recently joined. Yet the Depression was closing that world to it. Japan had been further humiliated by the naval limitations. It is not surprising that the Japanese turned in frustration to their past, to the ultra–nationalists, to the shining symbol that embodied their past. To the samurai.

* * * * *

The same year Prime Minister Inukai was assassinated, the U.S. Navy held its customary spring exercise off Hawaii. Admiral Harry E. Yarnell led his fleet on a mock surprise attack on Oahu. It was entirely successful. Perhaps Yarnell had been reading up on Major General Charles T. Menoher, chief of the U.S. Army Air Service who had predicted just before the Washington Naval Conference:

"Without control of the air, our entire force at Oahu will be practically helpless....The defenses of Oahu are concentrated in a rather small area and thereby are rendered vulnerable to well directed aerial attack. Having gained superiority of the air, the enemy might bomb at will the vulnerable points...."

Yarnell pulled off his coup by coming from the direction no one expected. From the north.

* * * * *

In a nation of tea ceremony restraint and courtly avoidance of the embarrassing, Gakko Tosho's 1990 junior high textbook is an Everest of

68

An artist's rendition of an assault on a hill at Port Arthur during the Russo-Japanese War.

Japanese forces during invasion of Manchuria.

understatement. Under the title "Confrontation of Japan and the United States," the Japanese schoolbook says: "The U.S. strongly demanded Japan's pullout from China. With cooperation of England and (the) Netherlands, the U.S. forced pressure (on) the Japanese economy."

This is true. What is left out is why, as the 1930s lengthened, the United States "forced pressure (on) the Japanese economy." Gakko Tosho could have written volumes on the topic. That this was not done was to eventually cause an uproar among Japan's neighbors about the writing — and rewriting — of history. Young readers of Gakko Tosho might start with 1934. In that year Tokyo gave two years' notice that it was ending participation in the Washington Naval Treaty and its limitations on warships — forty–three percent of the nation's budget was spent on armament. The following year, using as pretext the murder of a journalist in Tientsin, Japan forced China to remove all troops "objectionable to Japan" from surrounding Hopei province. Since all Chinese soldiers fit the definition, Japan was free to set up the East Hopei Autonomous Region. This put Japan twelve miles from Peking.

While this flirted with naked aggression, it should be taken in context. China at the time was a twelve–course dinner of factions. Chiang and Chinese communists were squared off against each other. Then there were the provincial warlords, a mixed bag whose loyalties sometimes extended no farther than to whoever was lining their pockets. One warlord was Feng Yu–hsiang, known as "The Christian General" because he was one and baptized his soldiers by turning a hose on them as they marched past. Han Fu–chu was known as "The Good Governor" of Shantung because he only collected taxes no more than five years in advance. True, the Japanese had occupied Jehol province between Peking and Manchuria. But Governor Tang Yu–lin, a jocular soul, had sold out to the Kwantung Army for $9 million, much opium and safe conduct for his wife and concubines. Tang was a physical fitness buff who liked to impress by pulling back a one hundred and sixty pound draw bowstring of an ancient Manchu weapon. He chose not to do so against the Japanese, but one general's men did fight briefly, the "Great Wall War."

While the Kwantung Army was never above *gekokujo* (insubordination), Tokyo had no firm policy in China. The navy and army did not march to the same drummer. And warfare between the Kodo and Tosei factions neared a bloody eruption. Kodo wanted a one–party state under the army with Japan put on a war economy. In February 1936 it staged an armed coup in Tokyo by soldiers of the First Army. Forces loyal to the emperor overcame the mutineers. Their leaders were executed after bullseyes were painted on their foreheads. Tosei had won but the victory was pyrrhic for parliamentary democracy. The military invoked a long–discarded policy. Henceforth, only an acting general or admiral could join

Japanese soldiers marching from the Yasukune shrine in 1934.

the cabinet as service ministers. Since the government fell if even one cabinet member resigned, this gave the military a veto over the government.

On August 15, 1936, Prime Minister Koki Hirota closeted with Hirohito to outline Japan's foreign policy. It sought, he explained, independence of the Philippines, expansion into Dutch Indonesia, development of Manchuria and close cooperation with China. What was not clear then, and is not today, was to what extent, if any, the emperor encouraged Japan's growing belligerence. You can have it both ways, depending on which historian you read. As mentioned, the emperor in 1936 could trace his lineage back to an ambitious mortal who mated with the sun goddess. But the Japanese did not always attach semi–divinity to the throne. One emperor of centuries past made a living for his family as an everyday carpenter. Why the Meiji Restoration is called just that is because the reformers of that period "restored" the awesome mystique of the throne as a bridge to antiquity in a period of upheaving modernization. The emperor was a rallying point. Commoners were not permitted to gaze upon him. His thin, high, formal voice was called "the voice of the crane," coming from afar, on high.

The soldiers of Hirohito's army, regarding themselves as incarnations of the ancient samurai traditions, were rewarded with cigarettes bearing the imperial seal. They were smoked with reverence, the ashes and butt preserved. Japanese soldiers,

72

upraised bayonets and swords glinting in triumph, were wishing the emperor long life when they shouted "Banzai!"

Two months after Hirota had given Hirohito one message, the Japanese government gave Chiang Kai–shek another. It demanded that China declare a joint war on the communists of Mao Tse–tung, that Japanese advisers sit in all branches of the Chinese government, that autonomy be granted five northern provinces. An already sorely beset Chiang took refuge in procrastination.

Japan in November 1936 had signed the Anti–Comintern Pact with Germany against Soviet communism. But the Japanese General Staff decided to steer clear of Europe's growing strife. Italy had invaded Ethiopia. Civil war had erupted in Spain. Hitler had embraced Mussolini in the Rome–Berlin Axis.

Not surprisingly, the Kwantung Army, now commanded by a general named Hideki Tojo and nicknamed "the Razor" for his precise, hard-headed ways, felt differently. Tojo urged a preemptive strike to prevent a linkage between Chinese

Chinese soldiers fighting the Japanese near Shanghai in 1937.

communists and Russia and the partition of Manchuria between them. Tokyo said no. It still hoped to be friends with Chiang.

Such sentiments never made it across the Marco Polo Bridge.

* * * * *

The Chinese were slanderously given to dismiss the Japanese as "the monkey people." Notwithstanding, the Japanese were included in the Boxer Protocol after that uprising which gave foreign nations the right to station troops at twelve points between Peking and the sea, ostensibly to protect their nationals' interests. Japan saw its interests as so large it had stationed four tmes the number of troops allowed under the protocol. On the night of July 7, 1937, some of them were holding maneuvers in the vicinity of Wanping, also not included in the protocol. The troops belonged to the Tanake Brigade: three infantry regiments, a tank company and an artillery regiment.

To avoid the breath of an "incident," General Sung Che–yuan ordered the Wanping commander to shut the iron–studded gates of the walled town until "the dwarf people" had completed their maneuvers.

At the Marco Polo Bridge, built in 1194 and where two railroads intersected near the village of Lukouchaio, what General Sung feared happened. Shooting broke out. Who fired first at whom is not clear to this day. A Japanese soldier was killed. More shots.

Had Major General Kenji Doihara, a firebrand of the Kwantung Army, tried to provoke another Manchuria? Were Mao's men trying to start a Sino-Japanese war? Whatever, the Chinese Twenty–Ninth Army behind the walls of Wanping was attacked. In Peking, where the European colony had been dancing and drinking champagne at Le Grand Hotel de Peking, U.S. Military Attache Colonel Joseph Stilwell heard war planes overhead. He sent his assistant, Major David D. Barrett, to investigate.

When Barrett arrived at Wanping, he saw Japanese and Chinese soldiers shouting insults at each other over the walls. A dead Japanese lay on the ground. Colonel Chi Hsing–wen refused Japanese demands that he turn over officers responsible for the shooting. Instead, Chi was lowered from the wall in a chair to negotiate. No go. Within two days, one hundred and fifty thousand Japanese soldiers were marching into north China. How had they gotten under way so quickly if the incident at the Marco Polo Bridge was an accident?

The prime minister in Tokyo was Prince Fumimaro Konoye, a noble in whom East met West resulting in an enigma. He was a fastidious dresser, whether in

74

Western attire or a kimono. A child who had been kept on a leash to keep him from falling down, Konoye had grown to be an anti–privilege reformer who nonetheless revered old–time traditions.

Konoye cabinet hoped the incident could be settled between the local commanders who had been on good terms until the Japanese died of a heart attack. Meanwhile Konoye was under pressure from the army to send more troops to teach Chiang a lesson. Konoye did not dare risk losing face politically in view of a public outcry against Chinese treachery. He yielded. On July 17, not knowing because of poor communications that a truce had been cobbled together at Wanping, Japan demanded China cease sending troops to the area. Chiang was in a bind.

What was left of a Shanghai department store front after it was hit by a shell in August 1937. Nearly four hundred people were killed.

Emperor Hirohito during his enthronement ceremony on November 10, 1928.

"China's sovereign rights cannot be sacrificed even at the expense of war," he said. Colonel Ishihara, a principal of the Manchurian incident, had subsequently said: "The first soldier marching into China will only do so over my dead body." But now, head of army operations, he flip–flopped again and urged sending soldiers to prevent Japanese in China from being massacred.

Amid all the crossed wires, one man was plugged in. Chinese War Minister Ho Ying–chin told his old friend, the Japanese military attache in Nanking, Chiang's capital: "If war breaks out, both Japan and the Chinese Republic will be defeated and only the Russians and Chinese Communists will benefit. If you don't believe it now, you will in ten years."

When word of the local truce reached Tokyo, Konoye ordered the Japanese troops recalled. But fighting renewed July 25 at a railroad station at Langfang, about fifty miles from Peking. The local commander felt he had been sent "to chastise the outrageous Chinese" and did his duty. Konoye against his better judgment sent his troops forward again. The army assured him the Chinese "problem" — it had been promoted from an "incident" — would be "solved in three months." In Peking, Lieutenant General Kiyoshi Katsuki said the Japanese were launching "a punitive expedition against Chinese troops who have been taking acts derogatory to the prestige of the Empire of Japan."

Putting the best construct on things that he could, Konoye said his soldiers were bringing "a new order" to East Asia. The old League delegate, Matsuoka, was more blunt. "Japan is expanding. And what country in its expansion era has ever failed to be trying to its neighbors? Ask the American Indian or the Mexican how excrutiatingly trying the young United States used to be once upon a time." He also said Japan was fighting to save Asia from white domination and communism. "No treasure–trove is in (our) eyes —— only sacrifices upon sacrifices. The all absorbing question before Japan today ... is can she bear the cross?"

* * * * *

As one hundred and fifty thousand Japanese warriors swept through China they did not come with a cross. It was a sword, unsheathed.

Konoye's New Order came to be called by Japan "The Greater East Asia Co–Prosperity Sphere." In reality, it was an at times barbarous assault throughout the region that rivaled what Adolf Hitler had unleashed on Europe and was to permanently poison the minds of many who survived it against the Empire of the Rising Sun. It was a vicious anomaly that a nation which had closed itself off from the world for two–and–a–half centuries would awake to wage seemingly instinctive war upon war on its neighbors, near and far. General Iwane Matsui said on leaving Japan for China that he was not going to fight an enemy but came "as one who sets out to pacify his brother." He ordered his men of the Shanghai Expeditionary Force "to exhibit the honor and glory of Japan and augment the trust of the Chinese people." Matsui, in a statement to his men on October 8, 1937, declared: "The devil-subduing sharp bayonets are just on the point of being unsheathed so as to develop their divine influence." Matsui was to be hanged after the war for what his men did in the city of Nanking.

* * * * *

America, its pride stubbed by a calamitous economic failure, had drawn its two oceans around it like a comforter. It wanted no foreign entanglements, East or West. Americans viewed the Japanese with a patronizing conceit. The United States sold them scrap metal which the Japanese turned into cheap toys that didn't last beyond Christmas dinner. "Made in Japan" was a synonym for tin. They were funny–looking people who harvested pineapples in Hawaii, tended the white man's gardens in Pasadena, tailored his clothes in Tacoma.

What was overlooked was that the Japanese had built a first class navy. Their torpedoes were far superior to the American equivalent. For some reason, fortunately, they had not and did not make a superior submachine gun. But their aircraft were excellent. (They were given designations for the year in Japanese history in which they were designed. The outstanding Mitsubishi fighter which came out in the Japanese year 2600 — 1940 — was called the Zero.) The Japanese had a first line army of four hundred and sixty–two thousand with many more in reserve while the U.S. Army did rifle practice with broomsticks. The nation dozed in a vacuum of unawareness. Peaceniks such as the Lone Eagle, Charles A. Lindbergh, and senators such as William E. Borah and Gerald P. Nye called the darkening clouds none of America's business. One of the Americans who saw farthest was Franklin Delano Roosevelt. But he had delicate political antennae and trod lightly.

FDR's reaction to the outbreak of fighting around Peking was stronger in words than deeds: "When an epidemic of physical disease starts to spread," the president said, "the community approves and joins in a quarantine ... in order to protect the health of the community." Joseph Grew, the patrician U.S. ambassador in Tokyo who had been a schoolmate of FDR's at both Groton and Harvard, disagreed. No U.S. interest justified risking war with Japan.

In Japan itself, even the Imperial Navy had doubts about events in China, although the admirals were hardly dovish. Japan should maintain the status quo in Manchuria and China and avoid getting into a war of attrition with either the

Japanese soldiers on a housetop celebrating the capture of Tienyuehasu in China in 1932.

Chinese or Soviets. Japan's target should be the oil and rubber of Dutch Indonesia and British Malaya. To head off the army, the navy seized the island of Hainan off the southern Chinese coast and landed a detachment in Shanghai. But the army continued to move south into China and into its vast interior. After hard fighting, the Japanese entered Nanking on December 13, 1937.

* * * * *

For the first time, the camera had become an instrument of war. Its vivid pictures and the technology to transmit them swiftly shaped attitudes around the world. There was H.S. Wong's unforgettable candid of a battered infant squalling in the ruins of Shanghai. There were newsreels of Chinese refugees being machine–gunned in the back as they tried to flee Japanese soldiers.

Norman Alley, an American cameraman with Universal newsreels, was working at the Pukow railroad yards in Nanking December 4 taking pictures of hordes of refugees escaping the city. Planes with the red ball of Japan on their wings and fuselages swept in and began strafing. "The wretched fugitives didn't have a Chinaman's chance," Alley reported. "The bodies of mangled dying and dead were two and three deep in many places ... in this canyon of death."

Then Matsui's soldiers arrived.

They rounded up groups of fifty or so, forced them to dig a trench which became their grave as Japanese soldiers shot them into it. While officers looked on approvingly, Japanese soldiers used Chinese for bayonet drill. Civilians were herded together, bound, doused with kerosene and then torched. Women were gang raped. Japanese soldiers waiting their turn slaughtered the screaming children nearby. Japanese stormed the Red Cross hospital, ripped bandages and casts off the wounded Chinese inside, then hacked them to death and raped and murdered the nurses.

* * * * *

At least twenty thousand Chinese men of military age were massacred in Nanking. As many women and girls were raped and murdered, then mutilated. More than two hundred thousand civilians and probably as many as three hundred thousand were slain. It was, said U.S. military attache Frank Dorn, "senseless."

Dorn speculated on Japanese motives in his history of the Sino–Japanese war.

The Japanese soldier was "brainwashed to the pseudo–idealistic belief that his mission was essentially a crusade to liberate the Chinese people from oppression. The average Japanese soldier had been shocked at the rejections of his efforts at

Chinese searching the debris of their homes after the invading Japanese in July 1937.

liberation. ... The frustration over Chinese ingratitude and resistance to Japan's high purpose ... were transformed in his mind into a sullen urge for vengeance and violent action."

In dry acadamese, Edwin Reischauer wrote of the Japanese, whom he had long studied and lived among: "... in an unfamiliar situation in which their accustomed patterns of courteous conduct don't apply, they have sometimes reacted violently." The former U.S. ambassador to Tokyo and Harvard scholar also writes of the Japanese vision of the world. "We." And "They."

* * * * *

At least one other Japanese was dismayed by the events in China. He was Admiral Isoroku Yamamoto, vice naval minister. He stopped smoking cigars in silent protest and gave all his supply away. He foresaw a collision with the West coming and this unsettled him.

In New York, five hundred people, mostly women, marched down Lexington Avenue wearing cotton stockings in protest against Japanese silk. The movie theater newsreel clips told the shocking story. The League of Nations reported that the world was spending $11.8 billion a year on arms, a huge sum when champagne from France sold for $1.89 a bottle and a Detroit convertible cost $960. But the League's only response to the gathering storms in Europe and Asia was words. Futile words. The German military attache in China called the Japanese army "bestial machinery." The German ambassador offered to mediate between the two antagonists. Meanwhile, back in Berlin, Hitler was telling his aides that Germany's need for *lebensraum* could only be fulfilled by force.

* * * * *

December 12, 1937, was — remember it — a Sunday. These were nervous days for Americans in China. The embassy warned U.S. nationals to begin packing. Many sought refuge wherever the Stars and Stripes flew.

None was bigger than the 26–by–32–foot flags painted on the sun awnings of the American Yangtze river gunboat, the USS Panay. Cameraman Norman Alley had sought refuge aboard. So had Luigi Barzini, an Italian journalist who was to become a noted writer, and a colleague, Sandro Sandri.

Not everyone respected the sanctuary of Old Glory. Colonel Kingoro Hashimoto, head of a Japanese artillery unit and founder of the ultra–nationalist Cherry Society, had torn an American flag from its pole at a mission in Wuhu and stomped on it. His guns had also fired on a British gunboat, Ladybird. But many Americans stuck to their duty, as they saw it.

Japanese troops guarding a bridge in Manchuria in 1931.

On that Sunday, the crew of the Panay had just finished a stomach–filling meal prepared by the Chinese cooks. Some of the forty–nine enlisted men — it had four officers as well — had taken a ship's boat over to one of three Standard Oil river tankers Panay was escorting thirty miles upriver from Nanking. They stashed their beer there. The U.S. Navy was dry. Standard Oil was not.

Panay was one of seven gunboats of the Yangtze Patrol. The United States, Britain, France and Russia had been granted permission to patrol the river by treaty with the Chinese since 1858. Panay's function was to show the flag, and it was doing its job this Sunday and then some. Besides the huge ones on the awning, it flew its Sunday ensign, the biggest in its flag locker.

Panay was a low freeboard vessel, built in Asian yards and specifically designed for the muddy, fast flowing river. It was a handsome ship, white with varnished brightwork that would have caught admiring eyes at a Harvard-Yale crew race. It could make fifteen knots under a full head of steam, carrying two five–inch cannon and eight Lewis machine guns wherever American presence was warranted.

This Sunday it was anchored, as were the tankers. A number of civilians were on board, having left Nanking for the security of the flag.

Japanese soldiers searching for the Chinese in 1937.

That morning a Japanese officer had signalled Panay from the shore, swivelling a cannon in its direction to emphasize the intent to board. Hashimoto reportedly had directed Japanese gunners to fire on any ship on the river. Panay's skipper, thirty-nine–year–old Lieutenant Commander James Joseph Hughes, an Annapolis man who preferred a tight ship to a happy one, idled his engines in mid–river as a boat with a machine gun and about twenty armed Japanese led by a lieutenant made out from shore. The officer said in crude English he was coming aboard.

The Japanese demanded if Hughes had seen any Chinese troops and where. Hughes said the United States was observing strict neutrality and couldn't tell the officer anything. Rattled, the Japanese asked if he could search the Panay and the tankers for Chinese soldiers. Hughes said no and then, suddenly growing his short size until, Alley remembered, "he was about nine feet tall," he told the Japanese: "And now, would you kindly leave my deck."

The officer, without any warnings that the Panay was sailing into trouble, did so. Hughes moved upriver and the little flotilla anchored. Lunch was served. Afterwards, Chief Bosun Ernest "Swede" Mahlmann stripped and started some sack time in his bunk forward.

Navy Lieutenant Shigeharu Murata was flying his Mitsubishi 96 bomber on patrol that Sunday — 96 for Japanese year 2596, elsewhere 1936. He said later he was at eleven thousand feet leading two other 96s plus twenty–one dive bombers and fighters. Lieutenant Masatake Okumiya, flying a two–winged dive bomber, said he was told ten vessels loaded with Chinese troops were fleeing upriver from Nanking. The planes were armed with four–foot bombs, their noses painted red.

Seaman Stan McEowen was on deck on the Panay when he saw the planes begin to dive. "I guess these Japs don't know it's Sunday," he said. The first bomb hit at 1:38 p.m. Quartermaster John H. Lang didn't hesitate. "All hands take cover! We're being bombed!" Mahlmann bolted from his bunk, threw on a shirt and ran topside to a Lewis gun. Alley grabbed his camera and began shooting incriminating pictures of Japanese attackers at almost deck level.

On the bridge, the executive officer, Lieutenant Arthur F. Anders, Annapolis '27, had been left speechless by a shrapnel wound in the throat. He wrote his orders on scraps of paper and on the white enamelled bulkheads. The skipper had been seriously wounded. Sandri was as well, mortally.

As the proud little ship started to go down, machine guns firing continually, the planes strafed and set two of the tankers on fire. Two sailors and a captain of a tanker were killed. Abandon ship was ordered. As Panay's launches pulled away,

Japanese planes strafed them, wounding a sailor. The survivors gathered in the marshy reeds ashore as the gunboat settled into the mud.

Panay was the first U.S. warship ever lost to air action.

* * * * *

The message was terse, almost like one four years later that became famous. This one, too, was U–R–G–E–N–T, from COMMANDER YANGTZE PATROL to COMMANDER IN CHIEF ASIATIC FLEET in Shanghai.

"13 DECEMBER 1937 10:03 AM

"MESSAGE RECEIVED BY TELEPHONE FROM NANKING. PANAY BOMBED AND SUNK AT MILEAGE 221 ABOVE WOOSUNG. FIFTY–FOUR SURVIVORS. MANY BADLY WOUNDED ..."

The Panay survivors straggled through the Chinese back country until finally picked up by British gunboats Bee and Ladybird and USS Oahu. The Japanese sent a destroyer hurrying upriver with medical teams. A Japanese doctor treating Quartermaster Tom Spindle said he was "so sorry," echoing the reaction of many of his countrymen afloat and ashore. Spindle thought maybe the Japanese weren't so bad after all until he saw some machine gunning refugees attempting to cross the river near Nanking. Cameraman Alley watched in horror as a Japanese patrol boat cut a raft of refugees in half, then fire at the survivors in the water. American ships raced to the rescue despite Japanese warnings not to interfere.

In Washington, Roosevelt called in the British ambassador, Sir Ronald Lindsay. The president said their two countries should blockade Japan. Lindsay, "horrified," said it would mean war. On December 17 Roosevelt outlined a prospective quarantine of Japan to his Cabinet. A Navy court of inquiry sifted the evidence and called the attack "wanton." Radio intercepts, it said, indicated the attack had been planned by an officer aboard carrier Kaga.

Roosevelt pressed Britain for a quarantine. The Royal Navy was receptive, but Prime Minister Neville Chamberlain was not and declined to join a proposed international conference regarding "bandit nations."

The Japanese, meanwhile, sent an official apology to Washington, exquisitely timed to arrive Christmas Eve. Roosevelt accepted it.

In turn, the Japanese dismissed Rear Admiral Teizo Misunami, commander of the naval air group in China. Tokyo paid $2,214,007.36 in damages in what Frank Dorn wrote was "probably the fastest international claim on record." A delegation

The U.S. gunboat Panay in a photograph taken just minutes before Japanese planes bombed it and sent it to the bottom of the Yangtze river.

This picture of the Panay was taken as the boat listed just before sinking to the bottom of the Yangtze after it was bombed by Japanese planes.

of Japanese schoolgirls left a donation at the Navy Ministry in Tokyo for Panay survivors.

This did not mollify the American public, which was furious. The Dallas News said: "The very probable truth in the situation is that military jingoism in the Japanese army, feeding on a blood–whetted appetite, has reached the stage of truculence to which conquering armies are invariably prone."

To smooth the waters Roosevelt asked that thirty feet of Alley's footage not be shown in American theaters. They showed the Japanese planes at deck level. The Japanese said they never flew below eight hundred feet, saw no flags and attacked the vessels while they moved upstream, presumably carrying Chinese soldiers from Nanking. Sorry, no. They were all anchored.

* * * * * *

There were two footnotes to the Panay "incident." The Japanese asked that if Panay were to be replaced, could one of their shipyards please be allowed to build the new gunboat. Secretary of State Cordell Hull delivered a terse: "No."

Then there was Coxswain Maurice D. Rider of Panay and Southampton, Massachusetts. Four years later he was still in the Navy, serving on the battleship Arizona. In Pearl Harbor. Eleven former Panay shipmates were stationed there, too.

5
THE PLAYERS AND THE PLANNERS

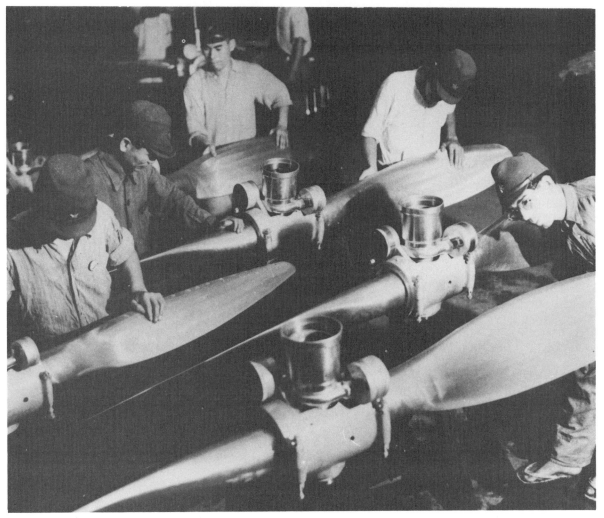

Workers inspect propeller blades at a factory in Hamamatsu, central Japan, October 1942. (Courtesy Mainichi Shimbun.)

For Isoroku Yamamoto and the casino at Monte Carlo, it was love at first sight. The roulette wheel of fortune. Chemin de fer. Baccarat. The rising young officer of the Japanese Imperial navy said that if something ever happened to his career, he would happily settle into the life of a gambler.

It would have been an odd, perhaps dishonorable choice for the son of a samurai. Yamamoto's father would have been a samurai had not that warrior caste been abolished by the Meiji reforms. The father was fifty–six when the son was born in 1884. Isoroku, an unusual name in Japan, translates as ten–five–six. Isoroku was subsequently adopted by the noted Yamamoto family, a common practice for well–born but impoverished parents. His new family enrolled him in the Japanese Naval Academy where he graduated in time to lose two fingers at the battle of Tsushima Strait.

Like many promising military officers, Yamamoto was sent abroad to learn and adopt the martial arts of the industrialized West. He spent a year at Harvard in 1919 where he was known as a convivial schoolmate who excelled at bridge and poker. His encounter with Monte Carlo in 1922 reaffirmed his love of the long chance. In 1926–28, Yamamoto was a naval attache in Washington. He became a great admirer of Abraham Lincoln through reading Carl Sandburg's biography of the president. He was equally impressed with America's industrial power in careful, note–taking tours of the assembly lines and steel mills of Detroit and Chicago.

Yamamoto was no less attentive to the court–martial of "Billy" Mitchell. After Mitchell had proved his point by sinking the target ship with bombs dropped from the air, he accused his superiors of "incompetency, criminal negligence and almost treasonal administration of national defense" for not absorbing the lesson.

Whatever the reaction among the Americans, Mitchell did make one fervent convert to air power: Isoroku Yamamoto.

90

Among the members of the Japanese cabinet which met with Premier Lieutenant General Eiki Tojo in Tokyo on October 18, 1941, were Shigenori Togo (left), foreign minister; Okinobu Kaya (center), finance minister; and Kunihiko Hashida, minister of education.

The young naval attache ran happy ships under his command, getting in nightly games of chess with his officers. But a naval attache's primary job is to look and listen, and it is highly likely he was familiar with the prophetic writings of one Hector Bywater, an English freelance journalist who specialized in naval affairs.

Bywater, whose work often appeared in the Baltimore *Sun*, covered the Washington Naval Conference. At that time he published a book, "Sea Power in the Pacific." It envisioned a surprise attack by the Japanese on the American fleet, key to the U.S. strength. The Japanese navy had first drafted a contingency plan for war with the United States in 1907. Japan's basic strategy called for luring the American fleet westward from its West Coast or Hawaii bases, sniping at it with submarines as it approached until ambushing it with overwhelming force as it neared the Home Islands. America's counter–strategy, embodied in a series of Plans Orange, finally stipulated a series of land fortresses across the Pacific to Guam and the Philippines bound together by a fleet always superior to Japan's.

Bywater's book was an instant best–seller among Japanese admirals. Translated as "Taiheiyo kaiken ron," it became part of the curriculum at the Imperial Naval Academy and the Naval War College. The idea of a daring surprise attack fit nicely with the steadfast injunction by Japanese naval theorists not to engage in a long war of attrition with America's superior industrial power. The leap from surprise to air attack was an easy one for a mind as nimble as that of Isoroku Yamamoto.

＊ ＊ ＊ ＊ ＊

The 1930s, as they neared their end, had become a train of powder burning shorter and shorter as it sputtered to an explosion. On March 12, 1938, German troops marched unstopped into Austria. On April 27, the Nazi party newspaper warned: "Jews, abandon all hope! Our net is so fine that there is not a hole through which you can slip." Later that year came Krystallnacht, a night of anti–Jewish terror for what Herman Goering called the Jews' "abominable crimes." That September, Munich became a symbol for appeasement when Britain and France agreed to let Hitler occupy the Sudetenland region of Czechoslovakia.

Half a world away, the Japanese had broken off any contacts with Chiang Kai–shek's Nationalist government, located in the interior of China at Chungking. China's only land access to the outer world was via the Burma Road over the Himalayas. Tokyo promised "complete extermination" of the Nationalists who "blindly persist in their opposition against Japan with no consideration either internally for the people in their miserable plight or externally for the peace and tranquility of all Asia."

Coming from the nation that had raped Nanking, this rang hollowly in the ears of the Western colonial powers. Their response accentuated the Japanese dilemma. The more aggressive the Japanese became in China, the more the Western nations talked of economic sanctions and hinted at military steps. And the more the island warrior people of Japan convinced themselves they were surrounded by enemies. And the more they saw justification of such conviction, the more they armed. And the more they armed, the more vital were the oil, rubber and bauxite of the colonies held by their supposed enemies. A vicious circle becoming more vicious.

Japanese and Russian troops fought a mini–war in 1938 along the Manchurian–Siberian border. The next year, the battle erupted again and continued for five months. Japan suffered fifty thousand casualties.

At the end of 1939, Japan's oil stocks had stood at fifty–five million barrels, enough to fight for eighteen months. Sixty percent of oil imports came from the United States. Japan's islands produced only twelve percent of the iron ore needed; the rest came from Manchuria with its hostile Russian neighbor. But the Japanese military remained split between those favoring a strike north against the hated Communist Soviet Union or south to grab the resources of Southeast Asia. The United States fleet remained an obstacle to both strategies. The navy stuck to

The translation of the Japanese caption for this 1941 or 1942 file photo reads: Neighbors meet to exchange ideas to save rice in Osaka. (Courtesy Mainichi Shimbun.)

its war plan of an ambush of the U.S. fleet in home waters. That way Japanese gunships could carry more guns and less fuel. But carrier admirals such as Yamamoto would need more oil to fuel far–striking carriers and their planes.

The hawks itched for action in either direction. Admiral Chuichi Nagumo disclosed his strategy to a dovish colleague, Admiral Shigeyoshi Inouye, who believed Japan should adhere to its Naval Treaty obligations.

"You're a fool," chided Nagumo. "I thrust with a dagger up under the ribs, and that would be it ...."

Germany's surprise invasion of the Soviet Union June 22, 1941, put blood in the water. Yosuke Matsuoka, now foreign minister, counseled: "When Germany wipes out the Soviet Union, we can't simply share in the spoils of victory unless we have done something. We must either shed our blood or embark on diplomacy.

The translation of the original Japanese caption for this December 12, 1942, picture reads: Braving winter winds, half-naked children of Hikawa National (elementary) School in Tokyo do physical exercises to harden their bodies. (Courtesy Mainichi Shimbun.)

It's better to shed blood."

An influential army colonel, Kenryo Sato, disagreed: "We gain nothing in the north. At least we get oil and other resources in the south." More cautious commanders warned that a southern strike would mean war with Great Britain. In the fall of 1940, as the Japanese began printing "occupation currency" for Malaya, Burma, the Dutch Indies and the Philippines, beleaguered Britain feared an imminent invasion of Singapore by the Japanese. Washington doubted this. And in Tokyo, U.S. Ambassador Joseph Grew cautioned against retaliation. "(This) would tend to push the Japanese people onward in a forlorn hope of making themselves economically self–sufficient." American Secretary of State Cordell Hull also favored prudence, at least until the United States was stronger in the Pacific.

On November 11, 1940, the German raider Atlantic captured the British steamer Automedon in the Indian Ocean. On board was a dispatch stating that Britain "must avoid an open clash" with Japan and would not go to war even if Japan attacked Siam (Thailand) or French Indo–China.

Presumably, this information was relayed by Berlin to Tokyo, as Japan had joined Italy and Germany in the Tripartite Pact of September 27, 1940. This storm–black war cloud had, however, a silver lining. It meant more top–secret radio traffic on the Tokyo–Berlin–Rome axis.

* * * * *

Of all the ironies about Pearl Harbor, one of the most pointed was aimed at the U.S. Secretary of War, Henry Stimson. A wise, measured aristocrat, Stimson had been Herbert Hoover's Secretary of State. He had been revolted when he discovered what Herbert Yardley had been quietly doing in his code–breaking Black Chamber. He closed it down with a bang — and one of the most famous utterances in all that occult craft: "Gentlemen do not read each other's mail." Ten years later, he was reading as much of it as he could get.

Yardley's crew had broken codes of nineteen nations by the time Stimson put them out of business. Yardley told all in a 1931 best–seller, "America's Black Chamber." Stimson, playing the innocent, said he had "never heard of such an organization."

Yardley's business philosophy as a code–breaker was simplicity itself. "Stud poker is not very difficult if you can see your opponent's cards." Americans had

Front page of the December 21, 1941, morning edition of Asahi Shimbun with the first picture of the Pearl Harbor attack, showing bombed Hickam Field by Japanese planes. (Courtey Asahi Shinbum.)

not been above taking a peek.

The alarm spread to Tokyo's code sanctuaries and they determined to make an unbreakable code. They came up with 97–shiki O–bun —— Alphabetical Typewriter 97.

Thomas Jefferson had been among those who presaged 97–shiki O–bun. He invented a machine with wheels that turned in sequence so that an "a," say, went in one end and came out "z" at the other. To decipher you had to find the key to the encipherment. Introducing electricity into the process one hundred and fifty years later meant the wheels could turn infinitely faster, producing millions of possible combinations. An electrical enciphering machine named Enigma was sold commercially in Germany after World War I. In 1927, the U.S. Army Signal Corps bought one for $144.

The Japanese had confidence in 97–shiki O–bun. The American eavesdroppers called the machine Purple after a color of the spectrum. They had already broken a

Japanese machine they called Red.

Captain Jinsaburo Ito of the Japanese navy had developed Purple, boasting: "Let America and Britain solve this cipher if they can." Washington assigned William Friedman, the onetime plant geneticist now of the Signal Corps, to give it a try.

Friedman's raw materials were literally plucked out of the air. The Japanese had used radio intercepting stations to pick up messages that the Russian fleet had arrived in the Orient to set up their triumph at Tsushima in 1905. In the 1920s the U.S. had set up listening posts for Japanese radio transmissions on Guam, Shanghai and the naval base at Cavite in the Philippines. Not only were codes intercepted, but by triangulation the posts could locate the transmitting and receiving Japanese warships.

Friedman's team of code breakers included stamp collectors, chess masters, math majors. This tiny, parochial world exchanged Christmas cards in cipher, held round–robin restaurant parties at which guests had to break an appetizer code directing them where to go for the fish course and so on through the menu.

Purple was for use only by major Japanese embassies. On February 18, 1939, Tokyo signalled these outposts that Purple was going on line. But it made a fatal error. The same message in Red was sent to lesser stations. Other little clues appeared. The Japanese, a formal people, stuck to proper and unvarying ways of address. Diplomatic messages delivered to American envoys could be intercepted and compared with their English translations.

For Friedman it was months of day in, day out, floor–walking sleepless night after night frustration. His wife, who had once broken rumrunners' codes for the Coast Guard during Prohibition, could only watch him suffer in silence.

"Naturally, this was a collaborative, cooperative effort," he said later (after a nervous breakdown). "No one person was responsible for the solution."

Commander Laurence Safford in the Navy's Code and Signal Section kept feeding intercepts. Safford had helped set up the radio spies in the '20s. In the finest tradition of interservice rivalry, his unit in room 2646 of the Navy Building had never communicated what it was doing to the Army Building next door on Constitution Avenue in Washington. Lack of communications was a crippling American handicap right up to the first bomb drop at Pearl Harbor.

Sometime in August 1940, one of Friedman's young cryptographers, Harry Laurence Clark, had an insight that came to him one night at home. He came to work the next day ecstatic. "I wonder if the monkeys did it that way."

"That way" was to use telephone stepping switches in the Purple machine instead of electric wheels. Friedman's crew began scrounging all available switches from the telephone company, even five and dime stores. They pieced together a copy of a machine none of them had ever seen — or ever would see — and which talked a language few of them knew. It buzzed and sparked and wasn't lovely, but on September 25, 1940, America's Purple machine decoded its first full message. The first two Purples cost $684.65. For that outlay Washington, again, could read Tokyo's hand. Even after the war, the Japanese refused to believe what Friedman & Co. had done. They said the Americans must have captured a Purple machine or stolen one. They had. Out of the air.

* * *

Purple was the machine. What it decoded was gathered under the rubric of Magic. Magic for the men and women — several key women — who decoded it all: magicians. The obvious question is why, with all this foreknowledge, the U.S. was ambushed at Pearl Harbor. The answer is equally and fatally obvious. In a word, no one person or groups of persons in one place was reading and interpreting what the magicians were providing. Nowhere was it all brought

"Dave," the Nakajima 95, a biplane fighter-reconnaissance float plane, similar to old U.S. Navy Vought Corsair.

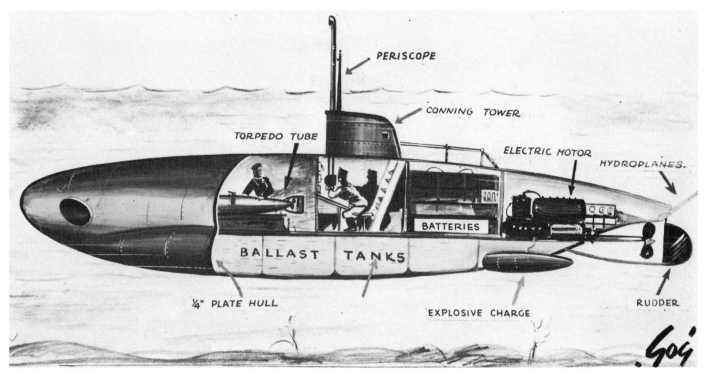

A two-man submarine captured during the Japanese attack on Pearl Harbor. It had a range of two hundred miles, forty-one feet long with a five-foot beam. It had a four-and-a-half-foot conning tower, and carried two eighteen-inch torpedoes. The submarine was carried on a mothership and launched about one hundred miles from the island.

The Nakajima 97, or "Nate," an older Japanese fighter. Top speed 250 mph at a 13,000-foot altitude. Maximum range 1,000 miles.

together and collated and analyzed and separated from all the conflicting radio "noise" which by itself often was just that but in a larger picture was an essential part of the landscape. Take the Navy.

Safford was chief of communications security under Rear Admiral Leigh Noyes, director of the navy's communications. Safford's job was to provide code and supervise intelligence security against snooping by foreign nations, particularly Japan. His staff of three hundred intercepted messages and decoded them through the translation section headed by Lieutenant Commander Alvin D. Kramer. He had a staff of three plus six translators. At another end of the Navy's organizational chart was the intelligence division (ONI) under Captain Theodore S. Wilkinson. Between them, that is between communications or codes and intelligence, stood the rub. This was the war plans division headed by Rear Admiral Richmond Kelly Turner.

Turner created a furious intra-service rivalry by insisting that war plans and war plans alone would interpret and disseminate what Magic was providing. He believed that ONI was made up of more junior officers who were trained to collect and distribute information but not to apply it to strategic situations. ONI was not to give any info to the fleet "which would initiate any operations." Example:

In May 1941 ONI concluded that the Japanese "will jump pretty soon." Turner vetoed that with a scowl: "I don't think the Japanese are going to jump now or ever!"

Turner had daily strategic estimates made up by his own war plans division. He did not show them to ONI. Wilkinson said he "had to learn primarily by way of the lower echelons what went on in Turner's division and what evaluation was put on the intelligence material (I) turned over to war plans ... We could only send information out without approval of war plans if it contained nothing but pure facts. We were prohibited from saying: "We invite your attention that this is a prelude to war."

Perhaps the most scrupulous study of pre–Pearl Harbor intelligence operations has been Barbara Wohlstetter in her book "Pearl Harbor: Warning and Decision." She wrote regarding Turner: "...When the job of collecting information is separated from the job of assessing its meaning, the fundamental motive or incentive for collecting information disappear." Since war plans was traditionally higher in the Navy's pecking order than intelligence, Turner "had no difficulty in monopolizing a function that was necessary to the effective performance of intelligence."

That was a structural problem. Then there were the mechanics. Magic was

NAVY
MacARTHUR NAME
"RUFE"

MITSUBISHI
"TYPE OO"

JAPAN

The "Rufe," a float type fighter.

about the most closely guarded secret in the nation's closet. To keep the Japanese in the dark that their mail was being read, intercepts from Cavite and elsewhere were sent by pouch to Washington by the weekly Pan American Clippers from the Orient. Which didn't fly when the weather was bad.

Then there was the scarcity of Purple machines. Cavite had one. Pearl Harbor's went to London instead in exchange for Ultra information. Lieutenant Commander Edwin T. Layton, intelligence officer of the Pacific fleet in Hawaii, wrote March 11, 1941, to his old buddy whom he had served with in Tokyo as language students, Commander Arthur K. McCollum. McCollum headed the Far Eastern section of ONI. Layton asked not to be shortchanged on any diplomatic intelligence pertinent to the Pacific fleet. McCollum wrote back:

"I should think that forces afloat should, in general, confine themselves to the estimates of strategic and tactical situations ... The political sphere is (not) ... determined by the forces afloat...While you and the fleet may be highly interested in politics, there is nothing you can do about it."

Layton's boss, Pacific fleet commander in chief Admiral Husband E. Kimmel, wrote in a similar vein from Hawaii to Admiral Harold R. Stark, chief of naval operations, on May 26, 1941:

"It is suggested that it be made a cardinal principal that CINCPAC be immediately informed of all important developments as they occur and by the quickest severe means available."

Stark was to testify at a Pearl Harbor hearing that he believed Kimmel was not only getting as much Magic as Washington "but was getting it sooner than we were." In truth, he wasn't getting any of it. What he did get were personal letters from the Navy's chief, one of which said "...the press on many of these points really gives you as much information as I have ..." Another, written twelve days before Pearl Harbor, gave his opinion on U.S. future actions:

"I won't go into the pros and cons of what the United States may do. I will be damned if I know. I wish I did. The only thing I do know is that we may do most anything ..."

Inter-service communications were even fuzzier if not totally opaque. Kimmel would get messages from Washington "assuming" he would pass the contents along to his Army counterpart in Hawaii, Lieutenant General Walter C. Short.

Perhaps the gravest omission centered on the Navy's "Hypo" decoding operation at Pearl Harbor run by Commander Joseph J. Rochefort who was perhaps the service's top codebreaker and who had studied in Japan and was fluent in the language. Hypo had been ordered in May 1941 — remember, it had no Purple machine — to concentrate on breaking Japan's so–called Admiral's code and its JN–25 naval operations code. The tragedy was that Hypo was told to ignore working on Japan's J–19 code. This was the code used by consulates around the world to communicate with Tokyo including the one in Honolulu. Hypo's J–19 intercepts from the consulate only fifteen miles away were forwarded undecoded to Washington (by Clipper) where, having a low priority, they piled up unread until more important traffic was deciphered.

It probably didn't matter when the Japanese freighter Nitta Maru docked in Honolulu March 27, 1941. But it did when one of its passengers came ashore. He gave immigration the name of Tadashi Morimura, an assistant–to–be at the consulate. His name was actually Takeo Tashikawa, an ensign in Japanese naval intelligence. He carried with him six $100 bills to cover expenses.

But the money came in handy to pay taxi driver John Mikami for driving him around Oahu to see the sights. A young nisei (second–generation Japanese–American) named Richard Masayuki Kotoshirodo who also worked at the consulate, sometimes drove "Morimura" around as well in his 1937 Ford. "Morimura" liked to go to the Shuncho–ro teahouse on Alewa Heights. The proprietress was from "Morimura's" home prefect. And the geishas helped him feel at home away from home. And on the lanai the teahouse had a telescope. There was a good view of Pearl Harbor with it.

6
POINT OF NO RETURN

An aerial view of Maui and its coastline, about one hundred miles southeast of Honolulu.

On January 27, 1941, in Tokyo, the Peruvian ambassador to Japan, Dr. Ricardo Rivera Schreiber, passed along some gossip he had picked up to a friend at the U.S. Embassy. The Japanese were planning to attack Pearl Harbor.

This was only days after Yamamoto had presented his proposal to do just that, a proposal wrapped in the tightest security. The source of the leak, or even if it was a genuine one, has never been traced.

Ambassador Grew passed it on to Washington for whatever it was worth. The news found its way to ONI, which concluded: "Based on known data regarding the present disposition and employment of Japanese naval and armed forces, no move against Pearl Harbor appears imminent or planned for the foreseeable future."

Touching all bases, however, ONI replayed the rumor to CINCPAC in Hawaii. The date was February 5, 1941, the very day Admiral Kimmel took over as commander–in–chief of the Pacific Fleet. McCollum of ONI's Asia Section advised: "Naval Intelligence places no credence in these rumors."

In short order, Kimmel had on his desk a report that was more than rumor. It was the work of Rear Admiral Patrick Bellinger, commander of the Navy's patrol planes out of Oahu, in collaboration with Major General Frederick L. Martin, head of the Hawaiian Air Force. The Martin–Bellinger report was completed March 31, 1941.

Said the report: "It appears that the most likely and dangerous form of attack on Oahu would be an air attack ... most likely launched from one or more carriers ... probably ... inside of three hundred miles." Martin–Bellinger recommended patrolling a 360–degree circle out from Pearl Harbor "as far as possible to seaward."

Commentary accompanying this Japanese newsreel picture described it as showing a Japanese plane taking off from a carrier to attack Pearl Harbor.

That was nice on paper, but Kimmel didn't have the planes available. The long–range PBY Catalinas under Rear Admiral Claude C. Bloch, commandant of Hawaii's Fourteenth Naval District, were needed for fleet operations, and there weren't enough to man a round–the–clock patrol anyway. The Army Air Corps had some four–engine B–17s, the Flying Fortresses which the Army was convinced, wrongly, would answer all its prayers. But General Short's responsibility, which he was to misinterpret, was the defense of Pearl Harbor. His planes scouted out only twenty miles. Deeper water was Bellinger's responsibility.

The day after the Martin–Bellinger report, on April Fools Day if anyone noticed, **ONI** alerted all naval districts that " ... past experience shows the Axis Powers often begin activities ... on Saturdays, Sundays and national holidays of the country concerned. ... Take steps on such days to see that proper watches and precautions are in effect."

Aerial view of Pearl Harbor in 1961, looking inland from the sea. Hickam Field is in the foreground.

Husband Kimmel ran taut ships as a cruiser and battleship commander where anchors were weighed to the second and spit–and–polish were rubbed in generously. A graying blond of fifty–nine, he was born in Kentucky and had long dreamed of going to West Point. He had to settle for Annapolis, graduating thirteenth in his class of sixty–two in 1904, the same year Yamamoto got out of Japan's Naval Academy. He served a hitch as the Navy's budget officer in Washington, earning a reputation as a straightforward, courteous Southerner. He dined afloat with his men, played a little cards with them, but preferred to study war plans in his cabin or curl up with a good book.

Layton, being fluent himself in Japanese, thought his commanding officer might be interested in a Japanese novel whose plot involved an attack on where they were talking, Pearl Harbor. Kimmel dutifully talked it over with his operations officer, Captain Charles "Soc" McMorris, a wise man as demonstrated by his nickname, short for Socrates. McMorris said the attack was possible but doubted Japan would run the risk.

Kimmel had other problems crossing his desk besides a novel. That spring the United States had figuratively crossed the Rubicon as to which ocean flanking it would get priority. The long range war plan, Rainbow 5, stipulated that the Atlantic and the fighting in Europe were the foremost concerns of the United States. Germany was enemy No. 1. The United States would take a defensive position in the Pacific, occupying islands in the Marshalls to the southeast of Hawaii and disrupting Japan's sea communications. As if to emphasize the point, the Navy in May transferred a carrier, three battleships and eighteen destroyers from the Pacific to the Atlantic where American vessels were to begin convoying Lend–Lease aid to Britain.

Army Chief of Staff George C. Marshall assured Roosevelt. Oahu, he said that May, was "the strongest fortress in the world." Any enemy approaching Hawaii would come under attack seven hundred and fifty miles from Pearl Harbor "which will increase in intensity until within two hundred miles (where) the enemy will be subject to attack by all kinds of bombardment closely supported by our most modern pursuit (planes)." With thirty–five Flying Fortresses in the islands, Oahu was "impregnable," Marshall assured the president, and "a major attack ... is considered impractible."

In fact, however, General Short had only twelve Flying Fortresses, six operational.

Short was sixty when he took the Army's Hawaii flag of command at Fort Shafter February 7, 1941. A native of Illinois, he had graduated from the state's university, fought in World War I and slowly rose through the ranks of the peacetime Army. He was not as fiery as Kimmel, whose messboys kept an old cap handy for whenever the skipper flew into a hat–stomping rage so he wouldn't crush a new one.

Short was an infantryman with his eyes on the ground, not the air. His view, updated by Hitler's use of dive bombers for his blitzkriegs across Europe, was that air power was used to soften up an enemy before moving in on the ground. In Short, writes historian Gordon W. Prange, there was "an obvious failure to understand or trust air power."

Kimmel was not without his resources. He had three carriers and eight battleships, but what to do with them was often not clear. Another letter from Stark to the admiral admitted the chief naval officer was as much at sea as Kimmel as to America's Pacific plans.

This picture, from a Japanese newsreel, was described as showing Japanese aircraft carriers en route to attack Pearl Harbor. Scene is from Japanese film obtained by the U.S. War Department and released to U.S. newsreels through the Office of War Information.

* * * * *

Alongside Hector Bywater's writings was another volume of required reading by Japan's military strategists. This was "When We Fight," by Shinsaku Hirate, written in 1933. It envisioned a Japanese attack on Pearl Harbor and became part of the War College course, "Strategy and Tactics for the United States."

Among Japanese fiction that same year was a novel by Lieutenant Commander Kyosuke Fukunaga, a novel whose title said it all: "An Account of the Future War Between Japan and the United States." Japan wins.

The book was shipped to Hawaii in hopes of sales among Japanese there. U.S. Customs agents confiscated it. The date of seizure was December 7, 1933.

Until November 12, 1940, such plots were only theories for Admiral Isoroku Yamamoto, now commander–in–chief of the Combined Imperial Fleet. On that date, twenty ancient, canvas–covered, Swordfish biplanes from the British carrier Illustrious attacked the Italian fleet in Taranto with torpedoes. Three battleships were knocked out of the war in the world's first successful carrier–based attack. The water in Taranto harbor was eighty-four to ninety feet deep. Pearl Harbor depths were only thirty to forty feet. Torpedoes dropped from a plane would sink in the mud. Or so it was thought. Until Admiral Yamamoto began thinking.

This was the same man who had said to Prince Konoye: "In the first six months of a war with Great Britain and the United States, I will run wild and win victory after victory. But then, if war continues two or three years after that, I have no confidence in our ultimate victory."

On January 7, 1941, Yamamoto submitted a nine–page outline of a Pearl Harbor attack to Navy Minister Koshiro Oikawa. A copy went to Rear Admiral Takijiro Onishi, the navy's tactical genius. Onishi gave the idea a sixty percent chance of success. He asked the opinion of Commander Minoru Genda, a brilliant naval aviator who had been an attache to London during the Taranto raid and had studied it intensively. Genda said it was risky but had "a reasonable chance of success."

Commander Tatsukishi Miyo, who served in the operations section of the naval general staff, was dubious. A Pearl Harbor strike would subtract from the carrier force needed for Japan's attack and occupation of Southeast Asia. Other negatives, Miyo was to testify after the war, were: "The degree of secrecy for such an operation would be difficult to maintain, the fact that the United States fleet might not be in Pearl Harbor at the time and the difficulty in securing proper intelligence for the execution of such an operation."

Yamamoto also brought his own operations officer, Captain Kameto Kuroshima, into the intimate circle of advisers. He was a distinctly un–naval type who could be found ambling about the flagship leaving smoke and cigarette ash in his wake. Then he'd retire with the bone of an idea to his cabin to gnaw over it in the dark, head in his hands. When inspiration came, he'd turn on the light and scribble furiously, oblivious of the dirty dishes and ashtrays piled around him.

Several imperatives were father to the plan. Time was running out as growing American reinforcements crossed the Pacific to the Philippines. So were Japan's oil stocks. There were also the matters of face and Japanese arrogance. Withdrawal from China in acquiescence to U.S. demands would be a disastrous loss of honor at home and abroad. And surely, many Japanese felt, their nation's "moral superiority" would win against the luxury–sated Americans, despite the odds.

Yamamoto had a more hard–headed reason for the attack. "Does anyone think for one second that we can carry out the southern operation without first crippling the American fleet?"

The chief of staff of the navy was Admiral Osami Nagano, who had studied engineering at Harvard, lived five years in the States and considered New York City his second home. He was to say to Yamamoto's clique: "My judgment is not always good because I am old, so I will have to trust yours."

By April 1941, the plan had a name: Operation Z after Admiral Togo's signal at Tsushima. Vice Admiral Chuichi Nagumo had been made over–all commander of the strike force, the First Air Fleet. He was a torpedo expert, not a flier, but he had seniority. Rear Admiral Ryunosuke Kusaka, a calm patrician who practiced Zen, had flown across the Pacific on the German dirigible Graf Zeppelin and had commanded a carrier, was chosen as Nagumo's chief of staff. Rear Admiral Tamon Yamaguchi, a combative graduate of Princeton, was named head of the Second Carrier Division behind Nagumo's First Division. Commander Takayasa Arima, who had attended Johns Hopkins and Yale, was made submarine planner.

Kusaka had serious doubts the fleet could be refueled on the way to Pearl Harbor but was told by Admiral Shigeru Fukudome, the navy's operations chief: "Make it work." He turned over the entire plan to Genda and senior staff officer Tomatsu Oishi. Kusaka nonetheless took his misgivings to Yamamoto aboard his flagship, the battleship Nagato.

"You just call it speculative because I play poker and mah–jongg," said Yamamoto. "It isn't." Later, in private, he told the still–unconvinced Kusaka: "I

Planes lined up at Hickam Field before the attack.

An unusual view of the huge wing spread of the Army's B-17 four-motor bombing plane.

England's "Hell Cat" Boeing B-17 Flying Fortress.

understand why you object, but the Pearl Harbor attack is a decision I made as commander–in–chief."

Oishi detailed the over–all plan while Genda fine–tuned the aerial tactics. He had thought of such an attack since 1940 when he got the idea from a newsreel. He kept urging Nagumo to keep his mind open for not just one but repeated attacks.

"One attack only! One attack only!" the admiral insisted.

Fukudome tried to buck up Nagumo: "If you die in this operation, special shrines will be built in your memory."

* * * * *

On both sides of the Pacific there were those who believed — or at least hoped — that peace could be won without resort to war. These were the diplomats, some of whom still wore striped pants. One was Admiral Kichisaburo Nomura, who at six feet towered over his countrymen in more ways than one. He had been summoned from retirement at age sixty–four in November 1940 to be Japan's ambassador to the United States. If peace was the intent, it was a good selection, Nomura had learned to admire America at first hand when he was a naval attache

112

The two-man Japanese submarine that was beached on the Hawaiian island of Oahu during the Japanese attack on Pearl Harbor.

in Washington where he had become chummy with the Assistant Secretary of the Navy, Franklin D. Roosevelt. His new assignment was not enviable. While Nomura was still en route across the Pacific, Foreign Minister Matsuoka was adamantly insisting on Japan's Co–Prosperity Sphere for the Far East.

"We must control the Western Pacific ... We must request United States reconsideration not only for the sake of Japan but for the world's sake. And if the request is not heard, then there is no hope for Japanese–American relations."

Such rhetoric contrasted with the assurances Nomura had been given by his former navy colleagues that they would not permit a war with the United States. Japan wanted the United States to stop aid to Chiang Kai–shek. In return, China would be left independent but in "cooperation" with the Japanese. Washington wanted Japan to get out of China, period.

Hull and Nomura began negotiating March 8, 1941, and were to meet more than fifty times. The Americans tried to convince Japan that their actions in the Atlantic convoy run were defensive even when on April 10 the U.S. destroyer Niblack dropped depth charges on a U–boat it thought was attacking it. It was the first American shot of the war.

Hull outlined to Nomura what were to be known as his Four Principles: territorial integrity of all nations, noninterference in the internal affairs of other countries, equal commercial opportunity and the status quo in the Pacific. Washington would also like Japan to leave the Axis powers. Hull was to summarize Nomura's position as Japan not wanting war "unless the policy of increasing embargoes should force his government, in the minds of those in control, to take further military steps."

The Americans, of course, all the while were reading Nomura's instructions via Purple, what Herbert Feis in his detailed "The Road to Pearl Harbor" calls "the radar of diplomacy." Layton was to say that Purple translators were "untutored in the subtle nuances of diplomatic Japanese" so that Hull was confronted with language "far stronger than intended."

For anyone reading the signals out of Washington they were simply confusing. The British, with Singapore, Malaya, Burma and India at stake, kept asking what the United States would do if any of those colonies was attacked. Washington gave no ironclad assurances. No less successful were the Dutch, whose oil–rich East Indies were now a colony without a head, the Netherlands being occupied by the Nazis. American indecision created a dangerous vacuum but a necessary one for Roosevelt who was walking a tightrope between isolationists and America

Nightfighters, short-distance fighters.

Parts of five Japanese Zeroes are made into a plane for the United States.

A Zero fighter, otherwise known as "Zeke." Maximum speed 326 mph, with a high rate of climb and a service ceiling of 38,500 feet. Normal range about 1,290 miles.

Firsters and his own pro–British inclinations. Stark echoed the dilemma in a letter the year before to Kimmel's predecessor, Admiral James O. Richardson.

"Suppose the Japs go into the East Indies? What are we going to do about it? My answer is I don't know and I think there is nobody on God's green earth who can tell you ... Just remember that the Japs don't know what we are going to do, and so long as they don't know, they may hesitate or be deterred."

The Americans got a jolt when Purple message 192 from the foreign ministry in Tokyo to Nomura May 5, 1941, was decoded. "Almost certain the U.S. Government is reading your code messages," it read. Two weeks later Nomura Purpled to Tokyo confirming that "I have discovered the United States is reading some of our codes." Convinced they couldn't be broken, the Japanese continued using Purple.

Nomura's message may have been based somehow indirectly on an indiscretion by U.S. Undersecretary of State Sumner Welles who had tipped the Russians that decoded German messages indicated the Nazis were about to invade the Soviet Union. Otherwise Magic was more closely guarded than the gold at Fort Knox.

The Navy and Army alternated each month bringing deciphered Magic intercepts to the White House by a high officer. The Army even started bringing summaries instead of verbatim transcripts to Roosevelt after a memo referring to Magic had been found in the wastebasket of Roosevelt's aide, Major General Edwin "Pa" Watson. (Roosevelt himself was partially out of the Magic loop for a time, evidence against those who claim the president was a master manipulator of Pearl Harbor to get the U.S. into the war.)

What Magic could not divine was what was going on in the debates of Japan's military leaders back home. Had Magic been able to "bug" the Imperial Palace, it might have seen a deeper significance when Japan and the Soviet Union signed a five–year Neutrality Pact April 13, 1941. But a silk screen was in the way.

* * *

Partners in peace, partners in war. That was the German attitude towards Japan once Hitler had invaded the Soviet Union. He increasingly applied pressure on Tokyo that its role as a full–fledged Axis partner was to let loose at the British

The forward gun ports and bombardier's window of the B-17F, a long-range bomber, at an airfield in Texas.

Empire soonest. Tokyo hawks agreed for purely selfish reasons. If Japan didn't grab for spoils now, there wouldn't be anything left for the taking. The persistent question remained, however. Was there more to be gained by aggression south or aggression north? The Neutrality Pact with the Soviet Union in the spring suggested that the general staffs had decided. But that was before Russia had been invaded. Now the question was whether Russia could last the winter. If so, a southern grab would bring quicker dividends.

The army, already mired in a war-in-depth in the vastness of China, did not want another in the vastness of Manchuria and Siberia. The navy saw no future in a Siberian "incident." No oil there. And Japan had already been mauled badly in the border wars of 1938–39. A seemingly unconnected development helped force a decision. In June, oil supplies temporarily ran short along the East Coast of the United States. Fuel shipments from there to Japan were suspended. Interior Secretary Harold Ickes, a man of strong opinions and actions, wanted to cut off Japan from American oil altogether. Hull said no. But fence–sitters in Tokyo got the message.

The Japanese had been twisting the arm of the Dutch in the East Indies to allow them greater control of their raw materials. Despite being without a homeland to call their own, the feisty Hollanders in Jakarta yielded only to the extent of promising Japan enough oil, rubber and bauxite for their normal consumption but no more.

The Japanese had also pressured the French, who, too, had only the pro–German puppet state of the Vichy government to call home, to let them use air bases in northern Indo–China, the better to strangle the Chinese. Now the Japanese wanted more, in south Indo–China. It was in that atmosphere that the military leaders began meeting in liaison conferences at Hirohito's Imperial Palace to decide Japan's future course.

The culminating session occurred July 2, 1941, with the emperor sitting impassively on his raised dais. The very presence of the emperor meant that whatever decision was reached became final. The president of the Privy Council, Yoshimishi Hara, argued as a devil's advocate in reality or out of protocol. "I do not think it wise for Japan to resort to direct, unilateral military action and thus be branded an aggressor."

Matsuoka told him not to worry. He would see to it that Japan did not appear to be the aggressor. Hara asked why the military did not go north as the people seemed to favor. "I want to avoid war with the United States. I don't think they would retaliate if (we) attack the Soviet Union." They might if Japan moved into

Indo–China, Hara feared. (At that juncture not even Roosevelt knew if he would, or at least the British and Dutch didn't know if he knew what he would do. Ditto Stark.)

War Minister General Gen Sugiyama said Germany was so powerful that not even an advance into Indo–China would provoke the United States to fight. His argument carried the day. The die was cast. Japan would move south. The emperor said nothing, which meant he said everything.

Prime Minister Konoye's records of the July 2 "conference" report that Japan "was determined to follow a policy which will result in the establishment of the Greater East Asia Co–Prosperity Sphere and world peace no matter what international developments take place...This will involve an advance into the southern region and, depending on future developments, a settlement of the Soviet question as well ... The Imperial Government will carry out the above program no matter what obstacles may be encountered." Japan would continue to try and settle the "China incident" and "seek a solid base for the security and preservation of the nation... In case the diplomatic negotiations break down, preparations for a war with England and America will be carried forward." The nation was to be put on a war footing and the army to draw up invasion plans for Malaya, Java, Borneo, the Bismarck Archipelago and the Philippines.

Point No. 3 of the conference decision declared: "In case the French Government or the French Indo–China authorities do not comply with our demands (use or establishment of air bases and naval facilities plus stationing of troops in south Indo–China), we shall attain our objectives by force of arms."

Purple readers in Washington had most of this by July 8. But the part about preparations for war with England and America had not been picked up.

Konoye, who was said to "carry long sleeves at (the Imperial) court," meaning he was a conciliator, was given a chance to continue negotiations with the United States "even at the cost of some concessions. The army also wanted Nomura to keep talking, at least until the fate of the Soviet Union became clearer. But there was an implied deadline.

Japan promptly informed Vichy that it would move into southern Indo–China July 24 no matter what Vichy decided. Vichy gave in. Sotomatsu Kato, the Japanese ambassador to Vichy, said France "had no choice but to yield." Nomura explained to Welles that Japan had to occupy Indo–China for its rice and raw materials and to defeat supporters of Charles de Gaulle still fighting under the French tricolor from London. Japan also acted, the ambassador said, to prevent Japan from "encirclement."

U.S. Army two-motored bombers (Douglas B-18) from Hamilton Field, California, flying over southern California in preparation for the Army's mass flight over the American Legion's National Convention Parade in Los Angeles in September of 1938.

Towards the end of July the emperor asked Admiral Nagano, he who was "too old" to make a decision about Pearl Harbor, what he thought America would do about Japan's move south. and could Japan win as it did in 1904 against Russia.

Nagano said he doubted Japan could win at all.

* * * *

Winston Churchill in a 1930 radio broadcast called the Soviet Union a "riddle wrapped in a mystery inside an enigma." He could further have encased Japan in a "puzzlement" as far as most Americans were concerned. Washington's military, being pragmatic Westerners schooled in might making right, greatly underestimated the Japanese character.

The newspaper *Mainichi Shimbun* editorialized after war broke out: "If we had been afraid of mathematical figures, war would not have started." The Japanese believed at home and abroad that will power would triumph over materialism. If not, death was a victory of the spirit. The Japanese believed that safety devices in

120

American warplanes were a sign of cowardice. A soldier who was captured had surrendered his worth, his humanity. That something like fifty-seven percent of POWs died in Japanese captivity during the war as contrasted to one to two percent at the hands of the Germans bears this out.

The Japanese were ironbound by a highly complex web of obligations and duties. Personal honor — face — was a paramount moral responsibility. It transcended the individual to the people as a whole. America's immigration restrictions, its relegating Japan's navy to second–place status, its intruding on Japan's "Imperial Way," were grievous insults that must be avenged. In her book "The Chrysanthemum and the Sword," anthropologist Ruth Benedict writes of the Japanese: "Evening of scores is not reckoned as aggression ... They need terribly to be respected in the world. They saw that military might had earned respect for the great nations, and they embarked on a course to equalize them. They had to out–Herod Herod because their resources were slight and their technology primitive."

General Sadao Araki, an ultra-nationalist, said in the '30s: ... "The true mission of Japan is to spread the Imperial Way to the end of the Four Corners. Inadequacy of strength is not our worry. Why should we worry about that which is material?"

Japan came upon its neighbors as an "elder brother" bringing protection and enlightenment. Too soft a hand might cause those to be enlightened in the Co–Prosperity Sphere to presume upon Japan's kindness to a pernicious degree. There was also the great influence of the emperor, to whom ultimate loyalty was due. No one could look on him from a second story lest he be higher than the most exalted one. A Japanese who once named his son Hirohito killed himself and his baby once he realized what he had done. The emperor's name was never to be spoken. But when he said nothing July 2, his silence meant "go."

* * * *

From his reading of Magic and other input, Admiral Kelly Turner of War Plans decided Japan would not go beyond Indo–China unless Roosevelt embargoed oil, as he had done months before with scrap iron in the face of continued Japanese aggression. Turner's advice was to keep the oil flowing.

Prime Minister Churchill met with his own advisers July 24 and told them he was convinced Japan would not fight Britain's empire until it was beaten in Europe. Japan did not want to fight Britain and the United States together, he said. In his biography of Roosevelt and Harry Hopkins, playwright Robert Sherwood wrote: "This conviction, shared by Roosevelt, was of enormous importance in the formation of policy prior to Pearl Harbor."

Speculation was agitated as to how Roosevelt would react to the Japanese occupation of southern Indo–China once it began July 24. FDR was at his estate in Hyde Park, New York, the next day but was not talking to the press. His news office in Poughkeepsie did so at 8 p.m. The United States was freezing Japanese assets in the United States. This meant no oil.

Feis writes: "The step had been taken which was to force Japan to choose between making terms with us or making war with us. No longer would the United States be providing the resources which left her [Japan] better able to fight if she should so decide."

The postwar Japanese, in rewriting history, say their nation was forced to react once the oil faucet was turned off or otherwise face strangulation. One might ask if the strangulation was not due to Japan's continued bellicosity which was a cause, not a result of the embargo ... or why Japan did not find its place in the world by peaceful economic means as it did in the postwar years, instead of such atrocities as the Rape of Nanking, the invasion of its neighbors.

History is often criticized as just a dull progression of dates. But some are significant. Japan all but decided on war at the July 2 Imperial Conference. The oil embargo came after the occupation of Indo–China July 24. Three weeks later.

* * * * *

On July 28, the Dutch warned Japan that if it did not conduct itself properly, they would exercise a complete economic blockade. They asked the Americans what they would do if Japan retaliated and invaded the East Indies. Washington hedged. The Japanese did not. Purple intercepted a message July 31 from the foreign ministry in Tokyo to Ambassador Miroshi Oshima in Berlin:

"Our Empire, to save its very life, must take measures to secure the raw materials of the South Seas. Our Empire must immediately take steps to break asunder the ever–strengthening chain of encirclement."

Hull got the decoded transcript August 4. It convinced him there was no possibility of agreement with Japan. Stimson said it demonstrated Japanese "duplicity."

But the talks went on.

7 NOISE

Boeing's B-17E bomber, chosen for mass production by the United States and Great Britain, offering a picturesque sight on a test flight in September of 1941.

In the summer of '41, hens around Kagoshima City at the southern tip of Kyushu stopped laying eggs. Farmers blamed the noise of so many planes flying overhead at all hours. Shoppers downtown instinctively ducked as warplanes roared past at roof–top level. Bystanders watched as the endlessly roaring planes headed towards a rock painted white out in the bay, then swiftly pulled up to circle and do it again. They did not know, nor did the pilots, that this was practicing to bomb Pearl Harbor.

Yamamoto had already held a theoretical war game for his brainchild. Theoretically he lost one–third of his aircraft and two or three carriers. This was acceptable. He was willing to lose half his strike force.

There was no end of details to master as well as practice, practice, practice. Lieutenant Commander Toshisaburo Sasabe, a navigation expert, pored over shipping patterns and reported back. Winter weather in the Pacific was so abominable above 40 degrees North latitude that commercial shipping avoided it entirely. It was rough but not as rough in December as it would be later in the winter when it would be impossible. Yamamoto duly noted this. Intelligence informed him the United States fleet usually held its exercises southwest of Hawaii towards the Marshall and Caroline Islands in belief that any attack would come from there.

There was a bomb problem. The Japanese models were light and would explode on contact instead of plunging deep into the innards of their targets. Genda got together with Commander Mitsuo Fuchida. They came up with a 1,600–pound armor–piercing naval shell converted to a bomb that would do the trick.

There was a torpedo. How to keep them from sticking in the mud instead of a battleship? No one had ever dropped a torpedo in only thirty feet of water. The

Japanese Ambassador Kichisaburo Nomura (left) and Japan's special envoy, Saburo Kurusu, as they arrived at the State Department on December 5, for a twenty-five minute conference with Secretary of State Cordell Hull.

Americans, in fact, thought it impossible and did not guard the battlewagons at Pearl Harbor with anti–torpedo nets. Yamamoto ordered a crash program of research. Not until November did they come up with the solution: wooden fins that prevented a deep dive. Meanwhile torpedo pilots practiced as much as twelve hours a day on an outline of battleship California painted on a beach. High–level horizontal bombers practiced over and over again until their bombs were on target seventy percent of the time. They found accuracy improved by flying into the wind to attack.

Dive bombers were a problem. The old models hit only forty-five percent of the time. The improved 99s raised this to sixty. Fuchida had been pleased at the accuracy of the horizontal pilots. He had doubted they would do no better than one hit in five.

Fuchida was a key man in it all, the man handpicked to lead the attack. He was thirty-nine, born in the Year of the Tiger, a symbol of strength. He had gone to the Naval Academy with Genda and specialized in high–level bombing. Genda thought him fearless. Fuchida had a mystical streak and admired Hitler enough to grow a duplicate to the Fuhrer's toothbrush moustache. Shigoharu Murata, who

Two intelligence analysts work at two Purple code machine analogs at the headquarters of the Army cryptanalysis service, in Arlington, Virginia, in 1944. The analog machines, devised by American cryptographers, enabled Purple-coded Japanese messages to be deciphered. The photo is courtesy of the Department of Defense.

Japanese pilots get instructions aboard an aircraft carrier before the attack on Pearl Harbor, according to the sound-track commentary accompanying the Japanese newsreel from which this picture was taken. The film was obtained by the U.S. War Department.

had bombed the Panay in 1937, was to lead the torpedo bombers. He was nicknamed Buddha for his good nature. "He would fly his bomber anywhere anytime," said an admiring Genda.

Yamamoto held another war game in September, factoring in a simultaneous attack on Malaya and the Philippines. This time he lost two or three of his carriers to as many American battleships. He was still not happy with Nagumo's selection as strike force leader who he thought was "given to bluffing when drunk, and he is not prepared even yet." But he had more pressing problems. Foremost was Hirohito. The emperor had spoken ambiguously the February before through his Lord Keeper of the Privy Seal, Marquis Koichi Kido: "I do not approve of anything in the nature of a thief at a fire. However, in dealing with the fast–changing world of today, it would not be gratifying to err on the side of benevolence."

Yamamoto's plan called for six carriers, to the horror of some admirals who thought this would monopolize his strike at the expense of air power for the southern attack. Acquisition of land bases in Indo–China stilled those fears.

In August an influential colonel in the war ministry, Kedeo Iwakuro, pleaded for sanity in the face of American superiority over Japan's resources: twenty-to-one in steel, one hundred-to-one in oil, ten-to-one in coal. Unheeded, he was transferred to Cambodia. On leaving he said: "When I return to Tokyo, if I survive, I'm afraid I shall find myself alone in the ruins of Tokyo station."

That same day Prime Minister Konoye asked for a meeting with Roosevelt proposing to withdraw all Japanese troops from Indo–China once the China "problem" was settled. Ambassador Grew endorsed the idea and warned Washington that Japan was capable of "sudden and surprise actions" and there existed "a national psychology of desperation (which) develops into a determination to risk all."

In September the emperor met with the military leaders and said diplomacy must be exhausted before armed action be taken. Navy Chief of Staff Nagano felt the pressure. Three days earlier he had told a meeting: "Each day we get weaker and weaker until finally we won't be able to stand on our feet. I feel sure we have a chance to win a war right now. I'm afraid this chance will vanish with time." Army Chief of Staff Sugiyama gave Konoye a deadline of October 15 for negotiations to work to avoid war. Operations plans were already complete for a simultaneous assault on Pearl Harbor, Hong Kong, Malaya and the Philippines. Sugiyama told the emperor the southern operation would be completed within three months.

Hirohito said he had been given the same timetable for the China "incident" and four years later it was still not settled. "Are you trying to tell me the same thing again?" he demanded of a cowering Sugiyama, his voice rising. "Can we absolutely win?"

Crestfallen, Sugiyama replied: "I wouldn't say absolutely... However, I will say that we can probably win. We'd rather not fight at all. We think we could try our best to negotiate and only when we're pushed to the edge shall we fight."

Nagano chimed in, even as he was awed by the loud voice and red face of Hirohito: Japan was like a person with a serious illness and only an operation could cure it. Otherwise it would slowly decline.

Sugiyama reminded the emperor that China was a large nation which would take time to conquer. "The Pacific is boundless," Hirohito replied tartly. He demanded if negotiation had the foremost priority. The soldiers stared at their feet. "Why don't you answer?" the emperor said to his stunned audience. Then they said yes.

Japan's minimum demands were to be an end to American and British aid to China, for them not to increase or reinforce their bases in Asia and for embargoes to be lifted and normal trade resumed. In return Japan would withdraw from Indo–China once the China problem was settled and meanwhile would not use it as a base for further expansion.

"If by early October there is no reasonable hope of having our demands agreed to by diplomatic negotiations, we will immediately make up our minds to get ready for war."

At the July 2 and September 6 meetings with Hirohito, the Japanese had twice gone to the brink but not quite over it. War was still not a unanimous choice. When Rear Admiral Takijirou Onishi, chief of staff of the 11th Air Fleet, was informed about Pearl Harbor in late September, he saw the consequences more clearly than anybody. Attacking the Philippines was one thing, he warned. But hitting Pearl Harbor would make the Americans "insanely mad." Kusaka bluntly told Yamamoto: "Your ideas are not good for Japan. This operation is a gamble."

"I like games of chance," answered the man who had been charmed by the bank at Monte Carlo.

This group of American citizens, all of Japanese descent, fill out landing forms on board the Japanese liner Tatuta Maru before they disembarked at Honolulu, October 23, 1941. The Tatuta Maru stopped there en route to San Francisco with several hundred American citizens being evacuated from the Orient.

* * * *

Potentially the weakest link in the long chain that led to Pearl Harbor was actually one of the strongest. This was the busy eyes of Ensign Yoshikawa, the ostensibly petty bureaucrat in the Honolulu consulate of Consul General Nagao Kita.

Presenting himself as a Filipino, he washed dishes at the Pearl Harbor Officers Club listening for scuttlebutt. He played tourist on a glass bottom boat in Kaneohe Bay near the air station where most of the Navy's PBYs were moored. He flew over the islands as a traveler. As a straight–out spy, he swam along the shore of the harbor itself ducking out of sight from time to time breathing through a reed. He was Yamamoto's ears and eyes. The Achilles heel of the whole operation was J–19, the consular code he used to send his information back to Tokyo. And Tokyo used to give him his instructions.

Rochefort, the codebreaker in Hypo at Pearl Harbor, besides being fluent in Japanese could decipher eighty percent of J–19 messages in about twelve hours. The most tell–tale of all was message 83 sent to Honolulu September 24, 1941. It instructed Yoshikawa to divide Pearl Harbor into a grid so vessels moored in each square could be pinpointed. This so–called "bomb plot" message was relayed to Washington by Clipper in undeciphered form. The Pan American plane had been delayed by bad weather so 83 wasn't decoded and translated until October 9 or 10. Washington had five times as many intercepts piling up for decoding from Manila than Honolulu because Manila was intercepting higher priority Purple. When he saw the decrypt of 83, Colonel Rufus Bratton, head of the Far Eastern Section of Army G–2 or intelligence, was brought up short. Never before had the Japanese asked for the location of ships in harbor. Bratton sent the message on to Brigadier General Leonard T. Gerow, chief of the Army's War Plans Division with General Marshall and Secretary Stimson marked in.

On the Navy side translator Kramer thought 83 an "interesting message." He testified later he was "under the impression" such messages were sent on to Kimmel in Hawaii. This one wasn't.

Captain Safford wanted it forwarded to Kimmel, but Admiral Noyes, Safford's boss, stopped him because he wasn't "going to tell any district commander how to run his job." Washington concluded the grid was simply a means of shortening Honolulu reports back to Tokyo and reflected the Japanese "nicety for detail." Navy colleagues assured Colonel Bratton: "When the emergency arises, the fleet is not going to be there, so this is a waste of time ... on the part of the consul."

Here is the crew of the sunken destroyer Downes, victim of the Pearl Harbor attack, as they appeared at the annual ship's dance held in San Diego in November 1939. All of the ship's officers and men except those required to remain on watch aboard the ship are shown with their guests of the occasion. In the circle is "Jack" Leo Stapleton, former gunsighter on the destroyer, who re-enlisted to avenge the deaths of his buddies.

G–2 head Sherman Miles was to testify that the bomb plot message alone was highly significant but that it was only one of many such. He conceded there were no other grid requests to any other American ports.

The basic problem was "noise" — too many radio signals out there in the airwaves, too many ears listening — and not always the right ears.

Long after the event a disgraced Kimmel was furious at not being told of 83. "No one had a greater right than I to know that Japan had carved up Pearl Harbor into subsquares and was seeking and receiving reports as to the precise battleships in that harbor ..."

Layton, Kimmel's intelligence officer, goes further in his memoirs: "The failure of the office of naval operations to ensure that the bomb plot messages were sent to us at Pearl Harbor was blind stupidity at the least, gross neglect at best...It is most unlikely that I or anyone else on Kimmel's staff would ever have dismissed the intelligence as merely 'a nicety of detail'...We never dreamed that Washington had been collecting Japanese intercepts that would have alerted us to the immediate danger far beyond any warnings of war we received from Washington."

A J–19 message to Honolulu from Tokyo on November 15 would have further cut through the "noise." This one asked the consulate to make a report of ships in harbor twice a week. It wasn't deciphered in Washington until December 3. Three days later Consul Kita was messaged to give grid locations of all ships at anchor and to transmit his reply with "great secrecy." That one was translated — in Washington — on Friday, December 5.

On October 23 the Japanese steamship Tatuta Maru docked in Honolulu. On board — he never went ashore — was Lieutenant Commander Sugura Suzuki of naval intelligence. Kita came on ship to brief him. He told Suzuki the United States had four hundred and fifty-five planes in the islands (actually there were only two hundred and twenty-seven including ninety modern P–40 fighters) and forty four–engined bombers (there were twelve, six flyable). Air patrols were few to none and all were in daylight. The ship soon set sail back to Japan carrying Suzuki to brief Yamamoto in person.

Contrast this to Admiral Bellinger who had forewarned of a possible Pearl Harbor attack in his March report. He said later he was never informed of any war warning messages from Washington. All he knew about U.S.–Japanese relations, he said, "came from the Honolulu newspapers."

Perhaps sensing intelligence coordination wasn't all it could be, General Gerow suggested on September 26 that a joint Army–Navy committee be set up to analyze information. Writes Layton: "Admiral Turner, like many naval officers of his generation, harbored a hearty distrust of his sister service. He disagreed." Miles was to testify: "Neither Gerow nor ... myself could get very far with (Turner)." The committee did not meet again until December 9.

* * * *

Perhaps the most damaging of all noises in the pre–Pearl Harbor cacophony buzzed inside Americans' heads. The noise told them in many ways that Japan was poised to leap. But almost to a man those responsible filtered out the signals that Japan would have the audacity, the skill to strike right in the solar plexus.

Nomura and Hull were still trying to patch together a peace. Roosevelt himself had warned the ambassador August 17 that the United States would take "any and all steps necessary" if Japan made any further moves towards "military domination by force or threat of force in neighboring countries." Privately the president complained to Hopkins that Hull wanted peace but couldn't be "specific" to the British and Dutch as to what the United States would do if their Asian possessions were attacked. It was, of course, the president's job to be

Minoru Genda told newsmen in London in 1959 that Japan should have crushed Pearl Harbor in 1941 rather than mounting a single attack. "We should not have attacked just once," he said. "We should have attacked again and again."

"specific." His refusal to do so drove Britain's ambassador to Washington, Lord Halifax, genteelly up the wall. Trying to pin Roosevelt down, he wired London, was "like a disorderly day's rabbit shooting." (In fact, it wasn't until December 3 that FDR finally guaranteed Halifax that Britain could count on U.S. "support" if attacked by Japan. And what kind of support might that be? Halifax inquired. "Armed support," said the president.)

Nomura, a man of honor, was having difficulty with whatever Konoye had up his "long sleeves at court." Purple picked up his plaint to Tokyo: "I don't want to go on with this hypocrisy, deceiving other people."

Hull would not back down from his Four Points. The Japanese softened their stand in a last ditch "concession" in November. They would get out of China — maybe in twenty-five years, which made it 1966.

When his October 15 deadline to conclude satisfactory negotiations passed, Konoye resigned. His replacement as prime minister was the "Razor" of Manchuria, General Hideki Tojo, who also took the portfolio of war minister. The army was now in the driver's seat.

Kimmel, to his surprise, was messaged from Washington that Tojo's apotheosis created a "grave situation. Take due precautions." Kimmel was not certain what such precautions might be. He was asked to and did pass the warning on to General Short. On October 17, CNO messaged Kimmel there was a "strong possibility" of a Japanese attack on the Soviet Union. In Short's view this "weakened" the chances of a U.S.–Japanese war. Inscrutable they may be, but the Japanese weren't crazy enough to fight both Russia and the United States and possibly Britain when they already had half a million men fighting a hot war in China.

Hull presented America's last offer November 26, a modus vivendi until something more permanent somehow emerged. Japan was to get out of China and Indo–China, then the two nations would talk some more, peacefully. Hull knew his answer before he made his offer. Nomura was stunned. The next day Hull threw in the towel, telling Stimson: "I have washed my hands of it, and (things are) now in the hands of ... the Army and the Navy."

Tojo's foreign minister, Shigenori Togo, testified revealingly after the war, in a way capsulating Japan's entire psychology of losing "face" since Commodore Perry:

"Japan was now asked not only to abandon all the gains of her years of sacrifice but to surrender her international position as a power in the Far East. That surrender ... would have amounted to national suicide. The only way to face this challenge and defend ourselves was war."

Herbert Feis in his book calls this reasoning "an absurdity. Japan was not asked to give up any land or resources except those which it held by force of arms." In Feis's western eyes, at least, there was "no warrant" for Japan to consider Hull's modus vivendi an ultimatum.

But by Japanese logic, the Empire of the Rising Sun was being encircled by enemies ever more tightly. Or was it that vicious circle of Japan's own making?

Former Japanese Navy Commander Mitsuo Fuchida, the pilot who flashed the code message "Tora, Tora, Tora" in the surprise attack on Pearl Harbor, died of diabetes in Tokyo at the age of seventy-three.

* * * *

Nomura had met with Roosevelt at the White House November 10. That same day, entirely unknown to the ambassador, Admiral Nagumo issued Striking Force Operations Order No. 1. All ships of *kido butai* were to complete battle preparations by November 20. It was the duality of this, girding for battle while talking peace, that was why Roosevelt was to call December 7 a day of infamy.

Nonetheless, as late as October the Navy was telling Konoye it really did not want a war with the U.S. But it was boxed in. If it said as much, it would lose face in public opinion which would touch off a dangerous encounter with the red hots of the army. Konoye approached Tojo, his war minister, suggesting the U.S. might agree to a limited occupation of China. The Razor was adamant. The army had fought too hard there to pull out now. Even dovish Admiral Onishi believed the army "could not be brought to its knees ... We should avoid anything that would put the army's back up too badly."

In late October, Hirohito was told of the Pearl Harbor plan for the first time. His reaction is unrecorded. (Even at the time of the attack only Tojo and the navy minister among his cabinet knew it was coming.) The few of the navy brass who knew gathered October 24 to celebrate in advance at the resort at Beppu. Yamamoto skipped the party.

In October Yamamoto had pulled his ultimate weapon against waverers. He sent his chain–smoking aide, Captain Kuroshima, to Tokyo to argue his case against those who wanted some carriers for the strike south. Kuroshima said if the fleet were divided, it couldn't reassemble in time to meet the American warships as they sortied across the Pacific. The Japanese flank would be bared. And if the admirals didn't agree, Yamamoto and his entire staff would resign. Rear Admiral Sadatoshi Tomioka, operations chief of the navy general staff, gave in. Only the emperor remained to be enlisted.

The supreme command spent most of he night of November 1–2 in debate. Hawks said the nation must maintain a protective position in China and negotiations to that end had failed. If American terms were accepted, Japan must submit to a disastrous peace. If it waited any longer, dwindling oil supplies meant a losing war. Tojo spoke: "Rather than await extinction it were better to face death by breaking through the encircling ring to find a way of existence."

Perry could have heard similar sentiments in 1853 if he had had a Purple machine picking up what chief counsellor Masahiro Abe told the shogun to do about the Black Fleet: "If we don't drive them away now, we shall never have another opportunity. If now we resort to a wilfully dilatory method of procedure, we shall gnaw out our navels afterwards, when it will be of no use."

Tojo and Sugiyama both told Hirohito that Japan would be victorious but added victory was irrelevant because Japan had to strike now or never.

The conference, however, decided to make one last try at peace even as *kido butai* was loading its new torpedoes, the ones with wooden fins that ran in shallow waters. The proposal was the one Hull turned down, the one about leaving China by 1966. The meeting set a new deadline for negotiations: November 25. After that, war. Hull's unacceptable counteroffer came, of course, the day after that. So, war.

* * * *

Operation Order No. 1 was one hundred and fifty-one pages long. It outlined the finely tuned attacks on Pearl Harbor, the Philippines, Guam, Wake Island, Hong Kong and Malaya. December 8, Tokyo time, was to be X–Day. The moon would be up from midnight to dawn, helping carrier operations. On the war's first day there would be strikes at twenty-nine targets: six on Oahu, ten in the Philippines, eight in Malaya, one on Guam, Hong Kong, Thailand and Wake. It was to go off like a string of firecrackers, ignited by two thousand planes, one hundred and sixty-nine surface ships and sixty-four submarines. Hawaii and the Philippines were to be hit at dawn. Since sunup came four hours later in Manila than Honolulu, the navy said it was a risk it would have to run that Clark Field in Douglas MacArthur's Philippine command would have advance warning. It hoped radio jamming would keep the news from reaching Manila.

Togo urged that for Japan's good name some form of advance warning be given. Nagano insisted surprise must not be compromised. The army wanted H–hour to be 1230 Washington time. The navy insisted on 1300 to give Hull time to read Tokyo's last message. That should take twenty minutes.

It was a brilliant plan in scope and timing, exquisite timing. Wrote Feis: "If the old tales are true, the Japanese take even more pride in their strategies than in their arms. The last resort of those with ends to gain — whether good or bad — was ruse and cunning."

On November 30 the emperor had one last question. The navy had always said it opposed war. Was it prepared? He was assured it was. Hirohito then directed Kido to tell Tojo to proceed as planned.

Even so, Tojo's navy minister testified after the war: "The navy was never confident of victory over the United States but we were confident that we were better prepared at that time to fight than we would have been at a later date ..."

"It was the forceful personality of Admiral Yamamoto rather than any rational argument that won over the naval general staff," says Barbara Wohlstetter.

Yamamoto. No one knew his enemy better. Wartime propaganda whipped up war fever in the United States by saying Yamamoto had promised to dictate peace to the Americans from the White House. That's not what he actually said. In a letter to a friend before Pearl Harbor he assessed the magnitude of the job ahead while also revealing the Japanese credo of death before dishonor:

"If hostilities break out between Japan and the United States," he wrote, "it would not be enough for us to take Guam and the Philippines, nor even Hawaii and San Francisco. We should have to march into Washington and sign the treaty in the White House."

Yamamoto had attended a ceremonial party November 13 for his senior officers at the officers club at Iwakuai Naval Air Station. The meal included sake, dried chestnuts, shellfish and seaweed, symbol of "to fight, win and be happy." Afterwards he bid farewell to Nagumo:

"I wish you godspeed and pray for your success."

8
TORA, TORA, TORA

Burning and damaged ships at Pearl Harbor.

On December 6, 1941, William E. Farthing was a colonel in the Army Air Corps. On December 8 he should have been made general of all he surveyed. Or a fortune teller.

In July that tall Texan, commander of the Fifth Bombardment Group at Hickam Field, completed an analysis of the use of bombers for the Army's primary mission in Hawaii: the defense of the naval base at Pearl Harbor. No one forecast the future more accurately. The Farthing Report stated: "The Hawaiian Air Force is primarily concerned with the destruction of hostile carriers in this vicinity before they approach within range of Oahu ... Our most likely enemy, Orange (Japan), can probably employ a maximum of six carriers against Oahu." Exactly Yamamoto's plan. Farthing's mind reading was even more uncanny. Or inspired.

"The enemy will be more concerned with delivering a successful attack than he will be with escaping after the attack. He will have carefully considered the cost of the enterprise, will probably make a determined attack with maximum force and will willingly accept his losses if his attack is successful.

"It has been said, and it is a popular belief, that Hawaii is the strongest outlying naval base in the world and could, therefore, withstand indefinitely attacks and attempted invasions. Plans based on such convictions are inherently weak and tend to create a false sense of security with the consequent unpreparedness for offensive action."

Farthing recommended Hawaii receive a bombardment force of one hundred and eighty four-engined plans plus thirty six long-range torpedo bombers "as soon as possible even at the expense of other units on the Mainland." The expense, the report stated, would be less "than the cost of one modern battleship."

Unfortunately, the United States had only one hundred and nine B–17s total. The bulk of them were slated for the Philippines and Britain and defense of the U.S. proper. Farthing's Report remained just that: a report.

The USS California at Pearl Harbor on December 7.

When he had hindsight, Farthing admitted: "I didn't think they could do it. I didn't think they had the ability."

The other prescient report, Martin's and Bellinger's in March had said a 360–degree long–range patrol was "desirable." Due to a shortage of aircraft and trained personnel "desirable" came to be interpreted as "when intelligence indicates that a surface raid is probable."

By late November "probable" seemed to have become an understatement. American radio range–finders picked up much traffic indicating active Japanese fleet movements. Purple decrypts disclosed Japanese embassies were being ordered to destroy coding equipment and classified papers. Kimmel was notified of this but was not galvanized by it. He had heard similar reports before.

"Soc" McMorris, Kimmel's war plans officer, said, "It was my opinion that (searches) would be largely token searches and that would give only limited effectiveness, and that training would suffer heavily and that if we were called upon to conduct a war, we would find a large proportion of our planes needing engine overhaul at the time we most required their services."

With the peace conference at an impasse, Washington's military on November 27 sent out a war warning to all points:"...an aggressive move by Japan is expected within the next few days ... either against the Philippines, Thailand or the Kra Peninsula (Malaya) or possibly Borneo. Execute an appropriate defense." The next day:"...Hostile action possible any moment. If hostilities cannot repeat not be avoided, the United States desires that Japan commit the first overt act ... (Do) not repeat not alarm the civilian population ..."

General Short interpreted the warning to prepare for sabotage from Hawaii's large Japanese population. He reacted like a westbound pioneer facing Indian attacks. He circled his wagons. Planes were bunched together so they could be more easily guarded. Ammo and fuel were removed so the aircraft wouldn't be as explosive.

PBY patrols began scouting to the north and northwest of Oahu out three–to–four hundred miles. Except Fridays and weekends. Then they were grounded for maintenance. Bellinger was saving them for action in the Marshalls and Carolines. He had eighty–one patrol planes including twelve on Midway Island, one thousand miles to the west. Fifty–four of those were new arrivals with partially–trained crews and no spare parts. The thirty PBYs available daily could only patrol forty percent of a circle. They concentrated towards Truk, to the west.

Admiral Bloch put near–in ships on submarine patrol with orders to shoot any vessels intruding in restricted waters around Pearl Harbor. Stark and Marshall agreed to reduce the fighter planes on Oahu to reinforce Wake and Midway. Carriers Enterprise and Lexington sortied from Pearl to deliver them. There would be no carriers in port December 7. The third Pacific carrier, Saratoga, was undergoing repairs stateside. All of Pearl Harbor's heavy cruisers and half its destroyers weighed anchor to escort Enterprise and "Lady Lex." In the Philippines, MacArthur was ordered to start sending some of Major General Lewis Brereton's long–range planes to scout Japanese bases on Formosa. The order was back–burnered.

Even at this late date signals were mixed. The Navy and Army in Washington sent separate war warnings to MacArthur and Asiatic Fleet commander Hart. General Marshall phrased his: "Japanese action unpredictable but hostile action

This Japanese Navy air view of smoking U.S. ships during the Pearl Harbor attack appeared in a 1942 Japanese publication called The New Order in Greater East Asia.

This Japanese midget submarine at Bellows Field was salvaged by a Navy crew.

The USS Maryland sustained slight damage, while the USS Oklahoma was capsized during the Pearl Harbor attack.

possible at any moment." Stark said it was "expected," not "possible." The services still didn't see eye to eye.

Ambassador Grew was as clear–minded as Colonel Farthing. In early November he counselled the State Department that if negotiations failed, he foresaw Japan "actually risking national hara–kiri to make Japan impervious to economic embargoes ... rather than yield to foreign pressure ... Japanese sanity cannot be measured by American standards of logic."

In mid–November Nomura had been joined by Saburo Kurusu, an able diplomat who had negotiated Japan into the Axis and had an American wife. Nomura–Kurusu continued the diplomatic blind man's bluff to, as Tokyo wired, "prevent the United States from becoming unduly suspicious."

Washington had no illusions. All Pacific commands had been messaged the day before Hull threw in the towel that "surprise aggressive movement in a direction (was possible) including an attack on the Philippines or Guam." Stimson confided to his diary November 25 as to "how we should maneuver them into firing the first shot without allowing too much danger to ourselves." (Japanese historians and American revisionists have jumped on this as evidence that Roosevelt was maneuvering his isolationist nation into war. This presumes he did at the risk of losing his Pacific fleet. And even if he was willing to take such an unimaginable chance, why wouldn't he have attacked the Japanese carriers — presuming he was so devious he knew they were coming — before they could attack him?)

On December 1, McCollum of ONI summarized the intelligence available. Consular officials in the Philippines and British and Dutch territories in Asia had been ordered to evacuate. Two large Japanese task forces had been spotted near

The close alignment of U.S. ships on Battleship Row in Pearl Harbor left them in a vulnerable position to the Japanese attack.

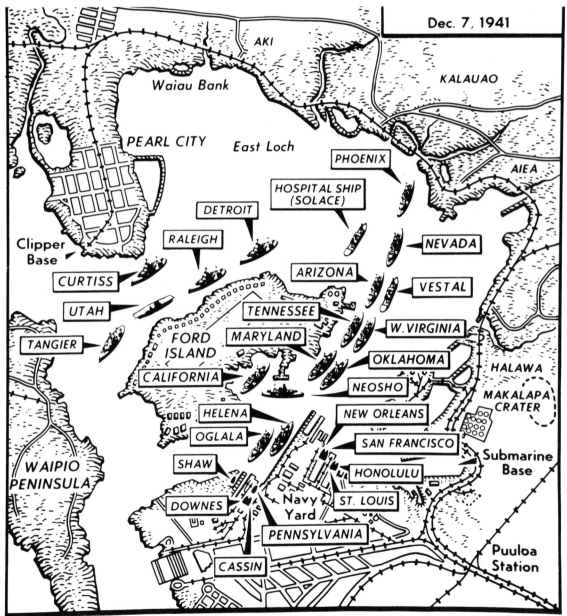

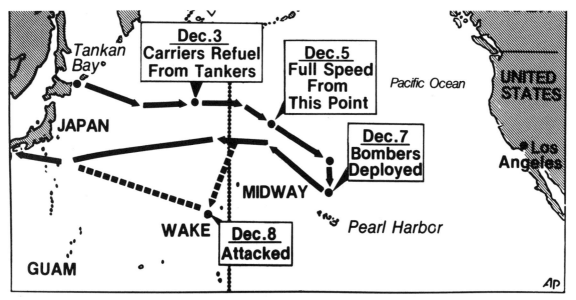

Ships of the Japanese Imperial Navy's combined fleet setting sail from Tankan Bay in the Kurile Islands, November 26, 1941. On December 1, the fleet received a coded message from Tokyo ordering the planned attack on Pearl Harbor. At dawn on December 7, six aircraft carriers launched one hundred and eighty-three planes of the first strike wave. On December 16, a task force parted from the main strike force heading south to Wake Island which was attacked on December 8 by bombers from the Marshall Islands.

While smoke rolls out of the stricken 31,800-ton USS West Virginia, a small boat rescues one of the battleship's seamen (foreground). Two men may be seen on the superstructure (upper center). The mast of the USS Tennessee may be seen beyond the burning West Virginia.

Formosa. Submarines were operating near Guam. McCollum asked if these forewarnings had been messaged to all points. Certainly, he was told. Not entirely, in truth.

On December 3 Kimmel was informed by Washington that Japanese embassies in London, Hong Kong, Singapore and Manila had been told to destroy their Purple machines. Kimmel asked Layton, his intelligence officer, what a Purple machine was. Layton said he had no idea.

Roosevelt was hand–delivered a Magic intercept November 30 sent by Purple from Foreign Minister Togo to Ambassador Oshima in Berlin advising him there was "extreme danger" that war would break out between Japan and the "Anglo–Saxon nations ... and the time of the start of this war may be quicker than anyone dreams."

On November 29 Purple decoded the so–called "winds message," a disguised weather notice that was to tip off Japanese commanders. "Nigashi no kazeame" — east wind rain — was to mean Japanese–U.S. relations were "in danger." American listening posts were put on the alert to pick it up. Safford was to say he did so December 4 or 5. Colonel Otis K. Sadtler of the Army Signal Corps wanted to send a message: "Reliable information (the customary euphemism for Magic) indicates war with Japan in the very near future. Take every precaution to prevent a repetition of Port Arthur (the 1904 surprise attack on Russia). Notify the Navy."

General Gerow rejected this, saying "the various departments have been adequately warned." Rear Admiral Royal Ingersoll, Stark's deputy, and Admiral Turner went to Stark's office to discuss further warning. They decided earlier alerts were sufficient. There was a danger of crying "wolf" once too often.

On December 6 Safford wanted to message vulnerable outposts like Wake to destroy their sensitive coding equipment "in view of the imminence of war." He told his boss, Admiral Noyes: "Admiral, the war is just a matter of days if not hours." Noyes replied: "You may think there is going to be a war, but I think they are bluffing." He agreed to let the message go, but not wanting to incur Turner's wrath, eliminated the "war imminent" part.

Of all the "noise," Barbara Wohlsetter was to conclude: "None of these signals was an unambiguous indication of Japanese intent to attack the United States ... However, even if the Magic signals were not unambiguous, they were at least good enough to provide a basis for decision. They indicated quite clearly a level of tension where an accident on either side could open a full scale war." Of the "winds signal" she says there was "no way on the basis of this signal alone to determine whether Tokyo was signalling Japanese intent to attack the United

Admiral Isoroku Yamamoto, who directed the attack on Pearl Harbor.

States ... It was only after the event that 'dangerous relations' could be interpreted as 'surprise attack on Pearl Harbor.'"

That Japan was moving to attack was indisputable. The two convoys had already been sighted heading for Kota Bharu in Malaya. An Australia spotter plane had even been shot down. There had been many signs amidst the noise. But none ever said in so many words that Pearl Harbor was a target. None. There had been years before a novel, a book by a stringer for the Baltimore *Sun*, even some prophets on the American side. But never in so many words. Never.

Indeed, as late as December 5 the Division of Military Intelligence concluded: "... They (the Japanese) want to avoid a general war in the Pacific..."

＊ ＊ ＊ ＊

The 1,500-ton U.S. destroyer Shaw, hit by three bombs and left a twisted mass of wreckage, had her forward magazine exploded by three bomb hits. Bow is lying on side in foreground. Part of the drydock at the right is under water.

After Ambassador Winant's urgent from London that the Malaya–bound convoys had been sighted, Kimmel asked his staff if he should sortie the fleet out of a potential trap in Pearl Harbor into the open ocean. No, it was decided. They wouldn't have cover from the absent carriers, the populace might be alarmed and it would be a drain on the fuel depots. So the fleet would spend the weekend in port as usual.

There was one last missed chance: Nagao Kita's consulate on Honolulu. On December 2 Kita was ordered to destroy his J–19 codes and transmit in PA–K2. Rochefort's Hypo station could decrypt PA–K2, but they were rusty at it. They didn't get around to deciphering Kita's PA–K2 messages for December 5–6 until after December 7. Thus they missed Yashimoto's of December 6, an implausible boner for a theretofore impeccable spy, the reddest of red flags even without hindsight. He had been updating Tokyo twice daily on ships in port for the last

This wreckage, identified by the U.S. Navy as a Japanese torpedo plane, was salvaged from the bottom of Pearl Harbor following the surprise attack by the Japanese.

week. On this Saturday as the clock ticked down, Yashimoto, who was ignorant of what was coming, or so he said, told Tokyo: "In all probability there is some considerable opportunity left to take advantage for a surprise attack against these places ... In my opinion the battleships do not have torpedo nets."

This was intercepted. It was sent to Washington for decoding. By Pan Am Clipper.

Yashimoto messaged Tokyo via RCA and MacKay Radio, alternating between the two services monthly. Both had refused to turn over dupes of the coded messages to American authorities. However, in mid–November David Sarnoff, head of RCA, visited the islands. He was persuaded to hand over the consulate's messages — groups of coded letters that Rochefort could break. Unfortunately, November was MacKay's month, so everything intercepted by radio was sent back to Washington.

For almost two years Captain Irving Mayfield, intelligence officer for Hawaii's Fourteenth Naval District, had had Kita's phones tapped. Early in December a

Damaged ships after the Japanese attack. The USS Casin (DD-372) and the USS Downes (DD-375) in drydock No. 1.

phone company lineman discovered the taps quite innocently and told the FBI. Discovered, Mayfield ordered them discontinued lest the news get out and he be blamed for an international incident.

One of Yashimoto's final efforts was the last message Tokyo sent out to *kido butai* December 6: "It appears that no air reconnaissance is being conducted by the fleet air arm."

* * * *

It makes a better story to say that Washington danced the night of December 6 away like the Duke of Wellington did on the eve of Waterloo. But it was in reality a nervous Saturday night along the network that was in on Magic. And for many who weren't.

The Navy's listening antennae at Bainbridge Island in Washington state began receiving Japan's final fourteen–point message at 0720 hours December 6. The first thirteen parts were teletyped to Washington by noon. They were in English,

Wreckage of the USS Arizona at Pearl Harbor.

so no translation was necessary. They said Japan had showed "utmost sincerity (*kido butai* had been at sea ten days) to insure the stability of East Asia and promote world peace (the Kota Bharu convoys were closing in on their targets)." The message accused Britain and America of conspiring with Chiang Kai–shek to foil solution of the "China problem". The United States had been "scheming" to extend war by "aiding Great Britain and preparing to attack in the name of self–defense Germany and Italy, two powers that are striving to establish a new order in Europe (34,000 Jews had been massacred by the Germans in September in a ravine in Kiev called Babi Yar)."

In Washington that afternoon Assistant Secretary of State Adolph Berle took his daughter to a matinee performance of "The Student Prince." He had read the first thirteen parts of Tokyo's message which obviously terminated the Hull–Nomura–Kurusu negotiations, and found them "insulting." He told his diary he went to bed that night "uneasy, the waltzes of 'The Student Prince' seemed like a dirge of something that may have existed once but certainly had very little relation to anything one knew today."

Washington slept.

Pearl Harbor slept.

Manila slept.

Kido butai awaited the dawn.

* * * * *

No one gets up earlier on a Sunday morning than a kid whose Dad had promised to take him fishing. No one hates to get up early on a Sunday morning than a Dad who had lived fully the Saturday night before. Thus it was that thirteen–year–old Peter Nottage was out on the lawn alone when he spotted some planes diving towards the Kaneohe Naval Air Station. They had red balls on their wings. Like any youngster living on the island fortress of Oahu in 1941, Peter Nottage was wise to things military. He figured the American fliers were holding another practice round between their customary Blue–Red teams, only this time the Reds had marked their aircraft.

Then his mother dashed out of the house. "This is war!" Mrs. Nottage and her son took a front row seat to watch the curtain rise on America's entry into World War II.

* * * * *

Bainbridge began picking up the fourteenth part of the Japanese message at 3 a.m. Washington time. It went off promptly to Washington.

"The Japanese Government regrets to have to notify hereby the American Government that in view of the attitude of the American Government it cannot but consider that it is impossible to reach an agreement through further negotiations."

Nomura was told: "Will the ambassador please submit to the United States (if possible the Secretary of State) our reply to the United States at 1 p.m. on the 7th your time. Please destroy at once the remaining cipher machine (Purple) ... also secret documents."

The Japanese were to consider this a declaration of war. To Barbara Wohlstetter,

A hastily constructed gun emplacement in front of Hangar 5 at Hickam Field was manned shortly after the attack.

"There was absolutely nothing in Magic that established such a Japanese intent (immediate war on the United States) clearly and firmly."

Lieutenant Commander Kramer had been on deck at the translation section of ONI and received the decrypt at 0800 hours. He noted the time for delivery and circled near–dawn time zones in the Pacific. Then he set off "on the double" for the White House to make delivery.

Colonel Bratton at G–2 read his decrypt of part fourteen at 0900. He became "frenzied." Sunday was a most unusual time for important diplomatic discussions. For a note to be delivered at a particular time and to a particular person, Hull, had never happened before. He reached G-2 head Sherman Miles at 1000. He also phoned General Marshall's home. The Army's commander was out riding his bay gelding King Story, accompanied by his pet Dalmatian, Fleet. They were somewhere on the government's experimental farm, future site of the Pentagon. His wife said the general needed relaxation. "My brain must be kept clear," he said. Bratton left a message for Marshall to call back. He couldn't detail over the phone because of security but it was "most important."

Marshall returned home, showered and told his orderly to get his stepson's red roadster. He met his own limousine coming for him and transferred, reaching the War Department about 1100. He began reading the whole fourteen parts while aides fidgeted. Miles thought the 1 p.m. time was "very unusual," but figured it was meant to be intimidating. General Gerow of war plans thought it all meant an attack on Thailand most likely.

Next door, at the Army Department, Captain Wilkinson, who'd been waiting for the fourteenth part in his office since 0830, considered the diplomatese "very serious, fighting words." It looked like an attack was timed for somewhere in the Far East, "and possibly Hawaii." He went down to Stark's office. "Why don't you pick up the telephone and call Kimmel?" Stark lifted the receiver: "No, I think I will call the president." The White House said he was busy.

Over at State, Hull was meeting with Stimson and Knox at 1100. Stimson recorded notes of the meeting: "Hull is very certain that the Japs are planning some deviltry, and we're all wondering where the blow will strike."

Hull began drafting an ultimatum to Japan that any movement close to the Philippines or south of 10 degrees north latitude "will of necessity be considered a hostile act."

Admiral Turner met with Stark at 1200, recognized part fourteen's "very great importance," asked what was being done, was told Marshall was preparing a message to the Pacific and considered that sufficient since the breakdown of negotiations merely "confirmed" the over–all situation.

Marshall's note said: "The Japanese are presenting at 1 p.m. EST today what amounts to an ultimatum. Also they are under orders to destroy their code machines immediately. Just what significance the hour set may have we do not know, but be on the alert accordingly."

Using the telephone could have compromised Magic were the Japanese somehow eavesdropping. Colonel Edward French, the Army's chief of traffic operations, said Marshall's message would take thirty or forty minutes to encode and transmit. Bad atmospherics prevented getting through to Honolulu. Instead, French chose Western Union's commercial telegraph rather than a "very fast" Navy radio. Marshall's warning cleared Washington at 1217 by teletype to San Francisco to be relayed from there by RCA radio. It was addressed to Army Commander, Fort Shafter and bore no priority.

In this panoramic view of Pearl Harbor, a warship is spouting, having been hit by a torpedo.

The original caption with this picture, received from Japanese sources in 1944, says it shows the burning of hangars at Hickam Field during the Japanese attack.

At the White House, Roosevelt had a 1230 appointment with Hu Shih, the Chinese ambassador. "This is my last effort for peace," the president said, showing his guest his message to Hirohito. His wife Eleanor poked around the door to remind him a family Sunday luncheon was upcoming. Hu Shih got up to leave. Roosevelt told him he expected "foul play," something "nasty" within forty–eight hours in Malaya, Thailand, the Dutch East Indies, "possibly" the Philippines. The ambassador left at 1310.

It was 0740 in Hawaii.

* * * * *

The moon was playing hide and seek with silvered trade wind clouds as the destroyer Ward patrolled a two–mile square off the south of Pearl Harbor. Minesweepers Condor and Crossbill were also out, brooming the harbor approaches. Condor's sharp–eyed officer of the deck, Ensign R.C. McCloy, spotted something off his port bow and called over Quartermaster R.C. Uttrick.

"That's a periscope, sir, and there aren't meant to be any subs in this area." McCloy blinked a semaphore to Ward at 0357: "Sighted submerged submarine..." Lieutenant Outerbridge, who got the command only two days before, roused his Minnesotan officers and crew with a General Quarters. He secured from it at 0435 having made no contact. Condor and Crossbill called it a night and the anti–sub nets to the harbor opened at 0458 to let them in. They weren't to close until 0840.

Meanwhile, Antares with its tow was waiting for a tug to come out and relieve her. At 1650, Antares' skipper, Commander Lawrence C. Grannis, saw something fifteen hundred yards off the starboard quarter and signalled the Ward. Outerbridge had turned in, was awakened and hurried to the bridge in a kimono. Looking through binoculars, he thought he made out a conning tower trailing Antares towards the harbor mouth and again sounded General Quarters. It was 0640 as the Ward closed to fifty yards and began firing point blank. Number 3 gun — it now stands in front of the Minnesota capitol in St. Paul — hit the conning tower, and the sub started to go down. Ward dropped four depth charges for good measure. At 0651, Ward radioed Fourteenth District headquarters: "We have attacked, fired upon and dropped depth charges on sub operating in defensive sea area." Unfortunately, the green skipper did not message that he had sunk a sub.

The Navy had three PBY Catalinas up on dawn patrol plus four others out of Kaneohe training with subs, plus five more scouting from Midway — four hundred and fifty miles to the east southeast to south by east, none to the north.

At 0700 Ensign William Tanner, flying one of the PBYs off Pearl radioed in code he had dropped depth charges on a sub and sunk it. At 0715, Admiral Bloch, head of the Fourteenth District, had been located and was inquiring if Ward saw a sub or shot at one. Meantime, Kimmel was reached at his home five minutes from his headquarters at the sub base in the harbor. "I'll be right down," he said. It was 0740.

Downtown, Tadeo Fuchikami showed up for work at RCA on his Indian Scout motorcycle to begin delivering telegrams. He cleaned out a pigeon hole for the Fort Shafter area including one addressed to the Army Commandant. Since it wasn't marked "urgent," he decided to fit it in on his regular rounds. It was 0733 when he set out.

It was 0702 out at the Opana radar station at Kahuku Point on the northern tip of Oahu. Privates Lockard and Elliott had been playing with their new toy. They had seen a lone blip between 0645 and 0700, phoned a report to control at Fort Shafter, been told to ignore it, but now Elliott saw "something completely out of the ordinary" due north at the set's extreme range, one hundred and thirty–seven miles. Watch officer at Shafter, Lieutenant Tyler, a fighter pilot, was on duty by himself and due off at 0800. He remembered a friend had told him a flight of B–17s was due in from the States. He had heard radio station KGMB driving in, and a friend had told him it stayed on all night for incoming planes to home in on. Lockard told him the green blip on his set "was the largest I've ever seen."

"Well, don't worry about it," Tyler said. Elliott wanted to get some experience time in, however, and kept tracking while waiting to be relieved by a pickup truck to take them to breakfast down the road. "It's a fine problem," he told Lockard... 0715, eighty–eight miles, three degrees of north ... Lockard took over because the blip was so large he figured the set was broken. At 0739 they lost the blip behind the hills of Oahu. The truck showed. They turned the set off to go eat. It was 0745.

* * * * *

At 0755, right on time, the "P" for Papa "prep" flag (blue border around a white square) was hoisted up the water tower of the sub base. Five minutes to go to morning colors promptly at 0800. On the decks of the battleship Nevada, the ship's band came to attention and prepared to play "The Star Spangled Banner." Some of those not looking at their music or the "P" flag noticed dots in the sky, planes coming in from the southeast, northeast, east and south. B–17s?

On shore, Fleet Chaplain William Maguire was waiting to go out to conduct Sunday service aboard the fleet. He turned to his assistant, Seaman James Workman, as both admired the new day: "Joe, this is one for the tourists."

P–40 pilots George Welch and Ken Taylor were still in tuxedos. They had come over from the fighter strip at Haleiwa to a dance at Wheeler Field and got caught up in an all–night poker game. They were debating whether to hit the sack or go swimming.

Seaman Leslie Short's thoughts were back home as he clambered into a machine gun station on the battleship Maryland's foretop to address Christmas cards. On the battleship Oklahoma, Quartermaster Jim Varner was plucking grapes from a bunch he tied to the springs of his neighbor's bunk just over his head.

Webley Edwards, manager of WGMB and host of the popular show "Hawaii Calls," showed up for his trick at the turntables with his own grapes — a can of grape soda.

The only vessel under way in the harbor was the destroyer Helm, heading up Naia Channel. A plane came skimming past at eye level. The pilot waved. Quartermaster Frank Hand waved back. Odd, unlike U.S. planes, this one had a fixed landing gear.

On the battleship California, a crewman saw red balls on the planes. "The Russians must have a carrier visiting us."

There were carriers, six of them, two hundred miles due north. On one of them, Admiral Chuichi Nagumo, in full uniform, listened intently to the radio for news of his "visit."

It was 0756.

* * * * *

When Akagi's navigator Gishiro Mirua reached his point on the chart, *kido butai* hove to. The cruisers launched four float scout planes. Two flew to the Navy's roadstead at Lahaina on Maui, the other to Pearl Harbor. One of them was the blip that Opana radar had picked up. At 0735 the Maui plane radioed: "Enemy's fleet not at Lahaina." The Pearl Harbor pilots reported some clouds over Oahu but Pearl Harbor was "absolutely clear."

The plane crews had been up well before dawn. They were issued box lunches: rice balls, pickled plums, chocolate and stimulant pills. Murata, the torpedo leader, put on red underwear. It wouldn't show blood if he were wounded. The pilots donned *mawashi* loincloths cinched with thousand–stitch belts. These were for good luck. Mothers, wives and sisters would stand on the street asking passersby

This remarkable combat photograph was made at the exact moment that the destroyer Shaw blew up during the Japanese attack.

to add a stitch until a thousand were sewn, each carrying a prayer for good luck and a good fight.

After a celebratory breakfast of red rice and red snapper, the crews headed for their planes. Nagumo ordered the carriers to head into a stiff wind at twenty–four knots. The ships rolled twelve-to-fifteen degrees in rough seas. Maneuvers were canceled when carriers heeled more than five degrees. Akagi launched eighteen Zero fighters, eighteen Val dive bombers and twenty-seven Kate level bombers. Within fifteen minutes, forty–nine bombers, fifty–one dive bombers, forty torpedo planes and forty–three fighters were airborne and fell in formation for Oahu. None of the pilots carried a parachute.

As the sun rose over the horizon, it honeyed the surf–fringed shape of Oahu. Lieutenant Toshio Hashimoto thought it was so lovely he snapped a photograph. Fighter pilot Yoshio Shiga had been to Pearl Harbor in 1934. He recalled happy memories.

Fuchida was to give two signals: "Tora! Tora! Tora!" (Tiger, Tiger, Tiger) if surprise had been achieved, then fire a flare indicating this. That meant the torpedoes were to be launched first before smoke and fire obscured the targets. But he thought his flare had been missed by some. He fired a second. The dive bombers misinterpreted this as indicating the Americans had been alerted and nosed down towards their targets.

As it turned out, the snafu didn't make any difference.

* * * * *

Far to the west, off Kota Bharu, Japanese warships began shelling the shore. It was 1 a.m., December 8 across the dateline, 0545 in Hawaii. Genda, who was with *kido butai*, knew the Malaya attack was to jump off two hours before his, but he had agreed to launch two hours later because his pilots objected to taking off in the dark. "I was resigned to leave our fate to Heaven," he said later.

Four destroyers and a light cruiser began shelling pillboxes held by the Ninth Division of the Indian Army. "Someone's opened fire!" the local Royal Air Force commander phoned Singapore. "Go for the transports, you bloody fool!" came the reply. General Arthur Percival phoned Malaya Governor Shento Thomas the news. "Well, I suppose you'll shove the little men off," said the nonchalant governor.

* * * *

Crews remove parts from a wrecked P-40. Of ninety-nine P-40Bs and P-40Cs on the island, seventy-two were damaged or destroyed during the attack.

Commander Logan Ramsey, Bellinger's operations officer, had been trying to confirm the PBY's report of sinking a sub when he saw a plane diving at Ford Island in the middle of the harbor. He thought it was some hot shot "flathatting" until he saw a bomb explode. He got on the blower: "Air raid Pearl Harbor! This is not a drill!"

There were ninety-six assorted warships and auxiliaries in Pearl Harbor that Sunday ranging from eight battleships, eight cruisers and twenty-nine destroyers down to the Baltimore, a survivor of Teddy Roosevelt's Great White Fleet, and mine layer Oglala which once did duty as a Fall River Line gin palace.

Many thought at first that some Navy or Army pilot was going to catch hell for dropping live ammo all over the place, but the truth was not long in dawning, Fireman Charles Leahey was easing himself in the head of destroyer tender Dobbin when Watertender Samuel Cucuk hollered at him: "You better cut that short, Charley. The Japs are here!"

162

帝國陸軍大學にて
東條博士―「後の故障は無視して
ボール・ハーバー丈けを覺えよ！」

This is a cartoon published in a Japanese language newspaper in Hawaii. It portrays Premier Tojo teaching Japanese a lesson on the blackboard emphasizing Pearl Harbor and minimizing any Allied successes in the war. The purpose of the cartoon was said to convey to Japanese in Hawaii the nature of the government of Japan and its Axis tie-up.

The body of a Japanese lieutenant who crashed during the attack on Pearl Harbor is buried with military honors by U.S. troops.

Private Frank Gobeo of the 98th Coast Artillery didn't know how to bugle call to arms, so he blew pay call instead. At Kaneohe a cook burst into Ensign Charles Willis's room beating a pan with a spoon crying over and over: "They is attacking!"

On the Nevada, the band played dutifully on with the national anthem even as torpedoes were splashing into Battleship Row and bullets tore up its ensign. When they finished, the twenty–three musicians ran for cover, then carefully packed their instruments in their cases except for a cornetist who crammed his horn into the shell hoist in his excitement.

For all the accumulating horror, the attacking pilots echoed the chrysanthemum and the sword of their culture. One remembered the bombs falling, falling until they were "as small as poppy seeds." Another thought they splashed "like a dragonfly laying eggs on the water."

Within minutes Oklahoma was hit by five torpedoes, West Virginia six, California two. Battleships Maryland and Tennessee were moored inboard and escaped the torpedoes.

The most murderous hit — and unluckiest of all — was the armor-piercing bomb that struck battleship Arizona near her No. 2 turret at about 0810. The bomb crashed through the deck as Genda had designed it and exploded into a fuel tank. Fire flared for seven seconds before reaching 1.7 million pounds of explosives. Arizona leaped into the air and settled fatally fractured into the mud with more than one thousand of its crew instantly killed with it. Some two hundred of them were later taken ashore and laid on the lawn in front of officers' bungalows, their blood soaking the grass red.

A battleship began turning turtle. "Looks like they've got Oklahoma," said Mrs. John Earle, wife of Bloch's chief of staff, who was watching in her yard on Makalapa hill. "Yes, I see they have," said her neighbor, Admiral Kimmel.

Across the way on Ford Island Esther Molter called to her husband Albert as he was beginning some fix-up: "Al, there's a battleship turning over."

Destroyer Helm was the only ship in the harbor under way, making for open sea at twenty–seven knots. Lieutenant Victor Dybdal could see the Japanese pilots waving. "For some reason we all waved back."

A Japanese pilot crashed into the harbor and fought off attempts to rescue him. Finally the crew from destroyer Montgomery shot him.

The duty officer on cruiser New Orleans ordered its dock hawsers cut loose. A crewman chopped through its shore power line instead. Ammo for the anti-aircraft guns had to be passed up by hand on the powerless ship. Chaplain Howell Forgy went below to help, uttering the memorable encouragement: "Praise the Lord and pass the ammunition!"

The B–17s from California flew into the war like drunks wandering onstage. Both Japanese and Americans fired at the unarmed planes. Some crash landed, one bellied down on a golf course, another managed to make it on the Haleiwa fighter strip. Welsh and Tyler, Tyler possibly the first pilot to go to war in tuxedo pants, had driven hell for leather to Haleiwa, gunned their P–40s without asking anybody and before they were through shot down seven Japanese between them. Lieutenant Homer Taylor brought his B–17 in and ran for shelter in an officer's house across the runway, hiding with the family under a sofa. He played yo–yo with a little boy grabbing his leg as he tried to run to the window every time a strafing Japanese roared by.

At Schofield barracks, Private Lester Buckley let all the mules out of the corral to give them a fighting chance on their own. Private First Class Joseph Nelles, Hickam chaplain assistant, ran back into the chapel to rescue the Blessed

This oil-stained, battle-torn, American flag was flying proudly from a captain's gig in Pearl Harbor when the Japanese struck. Battle missiles tore it from its staff and tossed it into the bay from where it was retrieved by Lieutenant Commander Fred Welden, who sent it back to the United States. It is being held by L.E. White (left) and Clyde E. Wilson, yeomen in the Naval recruiting office at Kansas City.

Sacrament just as a bomb hit, killing him. On destroyer Monaghan, Boatswain's Mate Thomas Donahue scanned the uproar quizzically: "Hell, I didn't even know they were mad at us." Seaman Short in Maryland's foretop dropped his Christmas cards and began spraying machine gun fire. A desk officer on another ship began throwing potatoes at the strafing planes in frustration. Daniel Inouye, a nisei senior at McKinley High School long before he became a U.S. senator, furiously pedalled his bike to help at an aid station. He looked up into the sky and said to himself: "You dirty Japs!" On cruiser San Francisco an engineer came topside to join Ensign John Parrott. "I thought I'd come up and die with you." Rear Admiral William Furlong stood on the bridge wing on Helena. A gunner called: "Excuse me, admiral, would you mind moving so we can shoot through here?" An officer playing golf went into a sand trap after his ball to find a soldier there shooting a rifle into the air. A bomb blew off a corner of a guardhouse. The inmates rushed out to help set up a .50 caliber machine gun. The phone rang in a Hickam hangar and someone reflexively picked it up. The caller wanted to know what all the noise was about. Kimmel stood in a window at his headquarters as a spent bullet tumbled in the window and hit him on the chest, smudging his whites. "It would have been better if it killed me," he said. Down the hall Layton, Kimmel's intelligence officer, caught sight of Admiral Pye, who the day before had said the Japanese would never attack the United States. He was wearing a life jacket, his whites smeared with oil, staring wordlessly into the middle distance. "Soc" McMorris appeared: "Well, Layton, if it's any satisfaction to you, we were wrong and you were right."

* * * *

Word reached the White House just about the moment Arizona blew up. Roosevelt was in his study with Hopkins who thought "there must be some mistake ... surely Japan would not attack in Honolulu." Roosevelt assumed "the report was probably true, just the kind of unexpected thing the Japanese would do and at the very time they were discussing peace in the Pacific they were plotting to overthrow it."

He phoned Hull at 1405 just as the first wave was leaving Pearl Harbor. When Nomura and Kurusu delivered the fourteenth part of the terminating message, he told the secretary "to receive their reply formally and coolly bow them out." The Japanese envoys arrived in Hull's office at 1420 Washington time. Embassy staffer Okamura's lack of typing skills had delayed their delivery. Hopes of presenting a declaration of war — although part fourteen never said as much — before the attack had failed. Pearl Harbor had already been under fire for an hour, Kota Bharu for two–and–a–half. Hull's rage was icy as he pretended to read a document Magic had already revealed to him. He had "never seen a document that was more crowded with infamous falsehoods and distortions so huge that I never imagined until today that any government on this planet was capable of uttering them."

As the stunned envoys bowed out of his office, Hull muttered "Scoundrels! Pissants!"

In Hawaii Webley Edwards broke into his platters at KGMB: "This is the real McCoy!... Those are real planes up there with red spots on them! Please believe me!" Then he returned to such top 10s as "Three Little Fishes in an Iddy-Biddy Pool." (Four years later Edwards came full cycle announcing Japan's surrender on battleship Missouri in Tokyo Bay). The Honolulu Star Bulletin had an extra out by 0930: "WAR! OAHU BOMBED BY JAP PLANES." The rival Advertiser ran out two thousand copies of its extra, then the press broke down.

In Washington Bill Peacock and Elton Fay were manning the desk at The Associated Press. It was to be somewhat more than a slow news day with new Soviet Ambassador Maxim Litzinoff due in town. The newsmen had just ordered peanut and bacon sandwiches from Whalen's drug store across the street. Fay

Two chief petty officers of the U.S. Navy, H.C. Abbas (left) and L. Precourt (right), place a wreath in Nuuanu Cemetery, Honolulu, as citizens honor the memory of men who died in the Japanese attack.

never got to eat his. At 1420, about fifty–four minutes after the bombs began falling, the phone rang. It was Roosevelt's press secretary setting up a conference call with Associated Press, United Press and the International News Service. "This is Steve Early. I am calling from home. I have a statement which the president has asked me to read: 'The Japanese have attacked Pearl Harbor, all military activities on Oahu Island.'"

Peacock swivelled his trembling hands to his typewriter and somehow managed a "flash," a priority designation: FLASH

"WASHINGTON––WHITE HOUSE SAYS JAPS ATTACK PEARL HARBOR"

Sunday, December 7, 1941, had become a day to remember.

Announcer John Daly broke into a CBS broadcast at 1431 prior to a 1500 program by the New York Philharmonic. He mispronounced it "O–ha–u." Paul W. Tibbetts, who one day was to fly over Hiroshima, heard it while twirling his radio dials flying his A–20 back from an exercise at Fort Benning, Georgia. He had simulated an attack on trucks bearing the sign "TANK." Listeners to Tuffy Leemans Day heard the bulletin just as the Dodgers scored on their way to a 21-7 triumph. But those in the stands remained ignorant unless they had remarkable insights as to why Colonel William Donovan had been asked to call his office immediately. Edward R. Murrow was getting in a late round of golf at the Burning Tree Country Club and assumed his dinner invitation to the White House that night would be canceled. "We all have to eat. Come anyway," said Eleanor Roosevelt. The phone rang at Fort Sam Houston in Texas. Mamie Eisenhower heard her brigadier general husband say: "Yes? When? I'll be right down." Some Americans simply couldn't believe it. At Pendleton Army Air Base in Oregon, Private First Class Ross Sheldon was a doubter until someone told him civilians downtown were standing men in uniform free drinks. "That clinches it," he said.

At the America First rally in Pittsburgh, Colonel Enrique Urrutia Jr., a Reservist veteran, demanded: "Can this meeting be held? Do you know that Japan has attacked Manila, that Japan has attacked Hawaii?" To cries of "warmonger," he was hustled out of the hall. "I came to listen," he shouted. "I thought this was a patriots' meeting, but this is a traitors' meeting!" The mood of the nation switched just as rapidly. Admiral Takijirou Onishi had been absolutely correct: Americans had become "insanely mad" at what they considered naked treachery.

The anger was to burn in some for half a century.

In Tokyo, Japanese gathered around loudspeakers and began clapping. They gathered outside the Imperial Palace bowing their heads in prayer. Hirohito penned his thoughts through Marquis Kido: Friendship had been the "guiding principle of our Empire's foreign policy. It has been unavoidable and far from our wishes that our Empire has now been brought to cross swords with America and Britain." Instead of declaring as pre–written that the war's purpose was "raising and enhancing the glory of the Imperial Way within and outside our homeland," Hirohito edited it to read: "... preserving thereby the glory of our Empire."

Prince Konoye heard the news on his radio and was crestfallen. "It is a terrible thing. ... I know that a tragic defeat awaits us at the end. Our luck will not last more than two or three months at most."

* * * * *

At Pearl Harbor, the second wave of the attack delivered another body blow from 0915 to 0945. Then the attackers flew off to the north. Opana radar, which had been turned back on at 0900, tracked the planes north but the Army didn't tell the Navy, which was sending its remaining planes looking for the carriers to the south and west. Fuchida was the last to land at 1300. He, Genda and others argued strenuously but futilely with Nagumo to renew the attack. The crucial oil tanks had yet to be hit. With them gone, the remaining American fleet would be powerless. But the admiral was adamant.

Kido butai turned for home.

Yamamoto put the operation in bridge terms. It was, he decided, a "small slam, barely made ... second–class thinking."

* * * * *

It is little remembered that there was a second Pearl Harbor. Ten hours after being alerted to the first, Japanese planes struck Clark Field in the Philippines, destroying one hundred and two planes, including all but three of General Brereton's B–17s. He had pleaded with MacArthur to attack Japanese air bases in Formosa. MacArthur replied through his aide, Major General Richard K. Sutherland, that he had been ordered not to make "the first overt act." What was Pearl Harbor if not an overt act? Brereton demanded. While the debate went on, the Japanese, at first delayed by fog, hit near high noon, finding MacArthur's planes neatly lined up in rows like the shooting gallery it was. "What the hell!" roared Air Corps chief Hap Arnold when he heard about it.

* * * * *

At 1458 in Honolulu, Tadeo Fuchikami finally made his delivery of Marshall's alert to the "Commanding General" at Fort Shafter. It was thrown in a wastebasket without carrying out the request to pass it on to the Navy.

"For a while I thought the Day of Infamy had been my fault," Fuchikami mused many years later. "Then I realized I was just one of the sands of time."

The Pearl Harbor attack had left eighteen warships sunk or damaged, including five battleships, and one hundred and eighty–eight planes destroyed. The raid killed two thousand four hundred and three Americans. The Japanese lost twenty–nine planes and fifty–five fliers. *Kido butai* returned home with three hundred and twenty–four surviving planes.

9
AFTERMATH

Memorial for Pearl Harbor Coast Guardsmen. Jeff Steinhem (center) prepares to throw a wreath into the waters of the Narrows, as an honor guard, (left) fires off a volley in memorial ceremonies commemmorating the twenty-third anniversary of the attack on Pearl Harbor. Ceremonies took place December 7, 1964, on the deck of the Coast Guard vessel Tuckahoe, as it cruised within sight of New York's Verrazano Bridge.

In the ruin and smoke of the aftermath, America began picking up the pieces. Housewife Kathy Cooper said: "If a Jap pilot walked into this house, I would have tried to kill him." Reporter Lawrence Nakatsuka checked out the Japanese consulate in Honolulu. Consul Kita didn't believe there had been an attack. Nakatsuka returned with a copy of the *Star–Bulletin*'s extra. Then the FBI arrived to find staffers still burning papers.

Rumors of treachery by Hawaii's Japanese population abounded. None proved true. The government did intern one thousand and four hundred forty–one Japanese residents, about as many as were already serving in the U.S. armed services on the islands. Trigger–happy gunners fired at anything and everything that Sunday night of uncertainty. A civilian was shot and killed when he reached through a miltiary fence to retrieve his hat that had been blown off by the wind. Two survivors of the Utah were machine gunned to death accidentally from the California. Oahu was blacked out, and one resident pondered how she could open the icebox without the light going on. A flight coming in from Halsey's Enterprise was shot at by friendly fire, killing five pilots, one as he parachuted to earth. Peter Nottage recalled he was never so frightened in his life as he walked with his mother up a darkened street to see his ailing grandmother and hear the clicking of a rifle bolt being closed.

"I never did get to go fishing that day," he recalled.

Amidst the rubble, the nation was already readying for war. At Kaneohe, where all but three of the PBYs had been destroyed, the order went out: the uniform of the day would no longer be whites but wartime khaki. The quartermaster didn't have enough to go around. So he had the whites dipped in boiling coffee.

The moon rose over the carnage of Pearl Harbor after midnight that Sunday. Those still up saw a lunar rainbow. By ancient Hawaiian tradition, it was a signal of approaching victory.

The shadow of a visiting Navy man falls on the battleship Arizona plaque commemorating the attack on Pearl Harbor. The plaque reads: "Dedicated to the eternal memory of our gallant shipmates in the USS Arizona who gave their lives in action, 7 December 1941. From today on the USS Arizona will again fly our country's flag just as proudly as she did on the morning of 7 December 1941. I am sure the Arizona's crew wil know and appreciate what we are doing — Admiral A.W. Badford, USN, 7 March 1950. May God make his face to shine upon them and grant them peace." (U.S. Navy photograph.)

* * * * *

When the war was over, John Toland, author of the Pulitzer Prize history of it, "The Rising Sun," interviewed Grand Chamberlain Nisanori Fujita of the Imperial Court. Fujita said Hirohito had told him:

"Naturally war should never be allowed. I tried to think of everything, some way to avoid it... The Emperor of a constitutional state is not permitted to express himself freely... If I turned down a decision on my own accord what would happen? An Emperor could not maintain his position of responsibility if a decision which had been reached by due process based on the constitution could either be approved or rejected by the Emperor at his discretion."

MacArthur as military ruler of occupied Japan allowed Hirohito to remain on his throne. Tojo was tried for war crimes and hanged. So was General Matsui of Nanking. Yamamoto was killed when his plane was shot down in an ambush — made possible by a Magic intercept. Congressional investigation after investigation pointed fingers at Kimmel and Short whose careers were blighted. Revisionists said Roosevelt had planned it all. Layton, who became intelligence officer to war hero Chester Nimitz, said in his memoirs there "is not a shred of evidence" that anyone suspected Pearl Harbor would be attacked.

The Japanese had made an immense gamble. They did not have a long–range plan nor did they judge the consequences of their surprise attacks.

The Pearl Harbor attack, the day Roosevelt called "a date which will live in infamy," changed the face that the United States turned to the world. Among its minutiae was the San Jose State football team. The war stranded them in Hawaii, so they volunteered for guard duty with the Honolulu police department. Quarterback Paul Tognett decided to stay on in the islands for good. After the war, he went into the dairy business.

FIFTY YEARS LATER

Time sometimes seems as entombed at Pearl Harbor as the barnacle–encrusted wrecks of the Arizona and the Utah in the waters off Ford Island.

The old coal docks and bunkers are still there. So is the red and white checkered tank that loomed over the Navy yard soon after the first drydock opened for business at the end of World War I. The duty day still begins with a blue "prep" flag rising on a mast atop the tank, signaling all ships in the harbor to raise their U.S. flags, just as on that fateful December Sunday when the twenty–three–piece band of the battleship Nevada, which had the duty, assembled on deck to play the national anthem as the first wave of Japanese bombers came through the cloud cover.

Off Ford Island's Battleship Row, Navy divers brought up a rusting Japanese torpedo bomb that failed to hit its target fifty years earlier. The lethal hardware lurked deep in the mud for half a century with its six hundred pound warhead still not detonated. A Navy demolition team took the torpedo out to sea and exploded the payload with a satchel charge one hundred and ten feet down on the ocean floor. The disarmed torpedo tube was fished up for display on the lawn of the Arizona Memorial visitors center. From time to time, harbor dredges scoop up a variety of war trophies: old airplane tires, props and struts.

Bartenders at the Pearl Harbor Officers Club, where destroyer commanders and their wives were billed $1 a head for that big Saturday dinner–dance on the eve of the Japanese attack, now frost up the mai–tai glasses well past midnight. The old territorial Sunday blue laws vanished decades ago.

Aerobics and weight control classes meet daily at the Bloch Arena, the old base receiving center where bands off the battleships and cruisers staged "The Battle of Music" on the night before the attack. Two decades later, Elvis Presley brought in $62,000 here at a benefit concert for the Arizona Memorial building fund.

Present-day Schofield Barracks, an officers club built before World War II.

Naval and Marine personnel of the aircraft carrier Bennington spelled out Arizona on the flight deck as it steamed slowly past the sunken battleship Arizona at Pearl Harbor. A total of 1,102 men stood at attention on big angled deck in respect for the 1,102 men who went down with the Arizona on December 7, 1941. The Arizona had 289 survivors. The Bennington, whose home port is San Diego, had been conducting operations in the Hawaii area. Hull of the Arizona is visible beneath the water. (U.S. Navy photo.)

Golf course at Kaneohe Marine Corps Air Station, along dunes where ancient Hawaiians were buried. The base was hit in both the first and second waves of the attack. A Japanese Zero landed near the course, its pilot buried temporarily in the dunes before his body was returned to Japan.

The man who led the Japanese attack on Pearl Harbor, Mitsuo Fuchida, returned to Hawaii a quarter century later, and recalled the events of December 7, 1941. Fuchida, his back to Pearl Harbor, points to where he led the Japanese planes through the mountains of Oahu Island, and down on to the crowded harbor where warships rode at anchor.

It was in the basement, "the dungeon," of the submarine headquarters where bandsmen off the California helped break the Japanese naval code after Japanese torpedo bombers broke up their battleship. Cryptographers found that these musicians' gifts for syncopation came in handy transferring the chords and ciphers of intercepted code messages to computer punch cards. An administration office on the second floor still contains the huge walk–in vault where the code–breakers stored their documents.

Japanese submarines and surface ships calling at Pearl Harbor these days are no more remarkable than the hundreds of Japanese tourists who daily follow the signs in Japanese and the upraised parasols of their tour guides to board the launches headed out to the ghostly white Arizona Memorial. Often wearing souvenir Arizona baseball caps, braided in gold, they listen in silence to the Park Service ranger's recital of how the bow of the great ship leaped out of the water before it settled to the muddy bottom in seven–and–a–half minutes.

Some of the harbor sightseeing boats that circle the monument deliver a bilingual speech, in English and Japanese, over their loudspeakers. Japanese pilots and navy crews sent to train at Hawaii's military bases often visit the monument in dress uniform, bow and salute fallen comrades, theirs and others.

More than a million–and–a–half tourists a year answer the bosun's pipe shrilly signaling the departure of the next launch out to the monument. Each week, nearly two hundred American flags, brought to the monument by patriotic and service organizations to take home as a treasured memento, are raised over the wreck of the Arizona.

Occasionally, some of the three hundred survivors of the sinking of the Arizona come to mourn and remember their entombed shipmates. Five times since the monument was dedicated on Memorial Day 1962, Navy divers have gone down to the wreck with the cremated remains of crew members who have died since.

Off Ford Island, wind–whipped whitecaps wreathe the rust brown submerged hulk of the USS Utah, where sixty–five names are etched on the lesser–known monument.

Cale Sterling, who was a pharmacist's mate at the base when the wounded and dead were brought ashore fifty years ago, today runs the officers club at Schofield Barracks. He lost his pharmacist's rating that morning and was demoted to ordinary seaman for handing out Springfield rifles from the supply room. Medics weren't supposed to touch weapons.

Along Nuuanu Avenue, past the Botanical Gardens, is the Japanese Consulate. Japan first opened a consulate in Pearl Harbor in 1885 after Hawaiian King Kalakaua, on a visit to Japan, asked the Meiji emperor to send settlers to work the pineapple and sugar plantations. In the gardens in the rear is a kukui tree planted by Emperor Hirohito when he visited Hawaii in 1975.

Today, with a $35 billion investment in real estate, banking and hotels, plus the influx of tourists each year, Japan is by far the biggest foreign player in Hawaii. Among the key investors is Mitsubishi, which during the war manufactured the speedy Zero fighter plane.

The Royal Hawaiian hotel is now Japanese–owned. It is dwarfed by the high–rise Sheraton Waikiki and its enormous shopping center, the Halekulani hotel, and a pair of outrigger hotel skyscrapers, all under Japanese ownership. In the past decade, Japanese investors have acquired a number of hotels, a couple of dozen golf courses, convenience stores and several office towers in the downtown business section.

The new generation at Hickam Air Force Base, which adjoins Pearl Harbor, is more apt today to show visitors a plaque marking the spot where Apollo 11 astronauts first touched earth after their historic flight to the moon in July 1969. The future seems to mingle easily with the past at Hickam. Its flight path is now pretty much taken up with the planes of the Hawaiian National Guard, which plays a key role in defending the islands.

At Fort Shafter, the softball field is named for Corporal Arthur Faureau, who was killed that fateful Sunday morning by strafing Zeros as he climbed the steps of the post chapel.

* * * * *

Of the ninety–four warships in Pearl Harbor on the morning of December 7, 1941, nineteen were sunk or severely damaged. But only the Arizona, the Utah and the Oklahoma never got back into action. The Arizona and the Utah rest where they were hit. The Oklahoma was raised and sunk again off Oahu to clear the harbor. The California was raised, repaired and refitted and took part in the reclaiming of Pacific islands by U.S. forces island–hopping toward Tokyo. The West Virginia, also sunk on Battleship Row, was back in action before the war ended. The Tennessee, moored beside the West Virginia and badly damaged, took part in the Pacific campaign. The battleship Pennsylvania and the destroyers Cassin and Downes all got back into action. So did the battleship Maryland and the cruisers Honolulu, Helena and Raleigh.

When the attack came, the Nevada was the oldest battleship in the Pacific fleet. Refloated and modernized, it got back into the war, took part in the Normandy invasion and closed out its career as a target ship in the Bikini atoll atomic bomb tests. The heavy cruiser Phoenix rose from the ashes of Pearl Harbor to win nine battle stars by war's end. It was later sold to the Argentine navy and was sunk by the British in the Falkland Islands war.

Two harbor tugs that survived the bombs and flames are still at work. The Wapello nudges ships inland out of the Panama Canal; the Hoge is employed by the city of Oakland, California. The Coast Guard cutter Taney, which was in Honolulu Harbor that day, is now in the Baltimore Museum.

Only two of the thirty–two Japanese surface ships of Admiral Yamamoto's task force survived the fighting in the Pacific. All six carriers that delivered the bombers to their target area were sunk by the end of the war.

* * * * *

At the end of the duty day, Navy personnel and shipyard workers are fond of going down to the yacht basin or the nearby small bar and restaurants to watch the sun sink into the Waianae Mountains above Ford Island. Outrigger canoes dart about in the channel. As dusk gathers, the Navy ships blink signals back and forth. Soft spotlights illuminate the Arizona Memorial; lights come on in the tall twin towers of the condominiums of Pearl City and in the homes rising on the Aiea Heights.

The serenity of the setting touches all.

Honolulu Star-Bulletin 1st EXTRA

8 PAGES—HONOLULU TERRITORY OF HAWAII, U.S.A. SUNDAY, DECEMBER 7, 1941—8 PAGES ★ PRICE FIVE CENTS

WAR!

(Associated Press by Transpacific Telephone)

SAN FRANCISCO, Dec. 7.—President Roosevelt announced this morning that Japanese planes had attacked Manila and Pearl Harbor.

OAHU BOMBED BY JAPANESE PLANES

SIX KNOWN DEAD, 21 INJURED, AT EMERGENCY HOSPITAL

Attack Made On Island's Defense Areas

WASHINGTON, Dec. 7.—Text of a White House announcement detailing the attack on the Hawaiian islands is:

"The Japanese attacked Pearl Harbor from the air and all naval and military activities on the island of Oahu, principal American base in the Hawaiian islands."

Oahu was attacked at 7:55 this morning by Japanese planes.

The Rising Sun, emblem of Japan, was seen on plane wing tips.

Wave after wave of bombers streamed through the clouded morning sky from the southwest and flung their missiles on a city resting in peaceful Sabbath calm.

According to an unconfirmed report received at the governor's office, the Japanese force that attacked Oahu reached this waters aboard two small airplane carriers.

It was also reported that at the governor's office either an attempt had been made to bomb the USS Lexington, or that it had been bombed.

CITY IN UPROAR

Within 10 minutes the city was in an uproar. As bombs fell in many parts of the city, and in defense areas the defenders of the islands went into quick action.

Army intelligence officers at Ft. Shafter announced officially shortly after 9 a. m. the fact of the bombardment by an enemy but long previous army and navy had taken immediate measures in defense.

"Oahu is under a sporadic air raid," the announcement said.

"Civilians are ordered to stay off the streets until further notice."

CIVILIANS ORDERED OFF STREETS

The army has ordered that all civilians stay off the streets and highways and not use telephones.

Evidence that the Japanese attack has registered some hits was shown by three billowing pillars of smoke in the Pearl Harbor and Hickam field area.

All navy personnel and civilian defense workers, with the exception of women, have been ordered to duty at Pearl Harbor.

The Pearl Harbor highway was immediately a mass of racing cars.

A trickling stream of injured people began pouring into the city emergency hospital a few minutes after the bombardment started.

Thousands of telephone calls almost swamped the Mutual Telephone Co. which put extra operators on duty.

At The Star-Bulletin office the phone calls deluged the single operator and it was impossible for this newspaper, for sometime, to handle the flood of calls. Here also an emergency operator was called.

HOUR OF ATTACK—7:55 A.M.

An official army report from department headquarters, made public shortly before 11 is that the first attack was at 7:55 a. m.

Witnesses said they saw at least 50 airplanes over Pearl Harbor.

The attack centered in the Pearl Harbor. Army authorities said:

"The rising sun was seen on the wing tips of the airplanes."

Although martial law has not been declared officially, the city of Honolulu was operating under M-Day conditions.

It is reliably reported that enemy objectives under attack were Wheeler field, Hickam field, Kaneohe bay and naval air station and Pearl Harbor.

Some enemy planes were reported shot down.

The body of the pilot was seen in a plane burning at Wahiawa.

Oahu appeared to be taking calmly after the first uproar of queries.

ANTIAIRCRAFT GUNS IN ACTION

First indication of the raid came shortly before 8 this morning when antiaircraft guns around Pearl Harbor began sending up a thunderous barrage.

At the same time a vast cloud of black smoke arose from the naval base and also from Hickam field where flames could be seen.

BOMB NEAR GOVERNOR'S MANSION

Shortly before 9:30 a bomb fell near Washington Place, the residence of the governor, Governor Poindexter and Secretary Charles M. Hite were there.

It was reported that the bomb killed an unidentified Chinese man across the street in front of the Schuman Carriage Co. where windows were broken.

C. E. Daniels, a welder, found a fragment of shell or bomb at South and Queen Sts. which he brought into the City Hall. This fragment weighed about a pound.

At 10:05 a. m. today Governor Poindexter telephoned to The Star-Bulletin announcing he has declared a state of emergency for the entire territory.

He announced that Edouard L. Doty, executive secretary of the major disaster council, has been appointed director under the M-Day law's provisions.

Governor Poindexter urged all residents of Honolulu to remain off the street, and the people of the territory to remain calm.

Mr. Doty reported that all major disaster council wardens and medical units were on duty within a half hour of the time the alarm was given.

Workers employed at Pearl Harbor were ordered at 10:10 a. m. not to report at Pearl Harbor.

The mayor's major disaster council was to meet at the city hall at about 10:30 this morning.

At least two Japanese planes were reported at Hawaiian department headquarters to have been shot down.

One of the planes was shot down at Ft. Kamehameha and the other back of the Wo ...

Hundreds See City Bombed

Hundreds of Honolulans who hurried to the top of Punchbowl soon after bombs began to fall, saw spread out before them the whole panorama of surprise attack and defense.

Far off over Pearl Harbor the white sky was polka-dotted with anti-aircraft defense.

Rolling away from the sea, huge spurts billowing clouds of soft black smoke transfixed a series of flares reddened the black expanse of the smoke.

Not from the silver-colored specks of the Japanese planes bombers scattered in battle formation against the high, incredibly blue sky.

Names of Dead and Injured

The city emergency hospital reported at 10:30 a list of 6 killed and 8 injured.

The complete list will be available. Here is a partial list:

Peter Lopez, 14, of 3801 Kamehameha St., was reported at 9:30 a. m. to be in serious condition, brought to the city emergency.

Service connected. 15, 1946 Kalihi St., is suffering from a mangled thigh, lacerations on the right leg and arm.

A Portuguese girl, unidentified, 16 years old, died on arrival from gunshot wounds.

Another victim who died on arrival was Frank Ohashi, 30, 736 Kamamalu St., from gunshot wounds in the chest.

Ursula Brodie, 8, Wooluiei Gardens, was released from the hospital after treatment for burns.

Three were reported injured and one reported killed from the bomb that fell at Fort and School Sts.

Schools Closed

All schools on Oahu, both public and private, will remain closed until further notice, Edward L. Doty, territorial director of civilian defense, announced at 11 a. m. to the brothers.

Editorial

HAWAII MEETS THE CRISIS

Honolulu and Hawaii will meet the emergency of war today as Honolulu and Hawaii have met emergencies in the past—coolly, calmly and with immediate and complete support of the officials, officers and troops who are in charge.

Governor Poindexter and the army and navy leaders have called upon the public to remain calm; for civilians who have no essential business on the streets to stay off, and for every man and woman to do his duty.

That request, coupled with the measures promptly taken to meet the situation that has suddenly and terribly developed, will be needed.

Hawaii will do its part, as a loyal American territory. In this crisis, every difference of race, creed and color will be submerged in the one desire and determination to play our part that Americans always play in crisis.

BULLETIN

Additional Star-Bulletin extras today will cover the latest developments in this war move.

The scene was chaotic at the Federal Office Builiding in San Francisco as young men enlisted in the U.S. Navy the night of December 7, just hours after war came to the Pacific.

Service men and civilians gather in a cigar store on Broadway in New York to hear President Roosevelt's address.

President Roosevelt, appearing before a joint session of Congress on December 8, terms the attack by Japan upon Hawaii and the Philippines as dastardly and unprovoked. He asks for an immediate declaration of war.

WAR EXTRA! WAR EXTRA!

U. S. FLEET IN ACTION

Destroyers Attack Jap Raiders

104 DIE IN HAWAII BOMBING

SUNRISE EDITION

Seattle Post - Intelligencer
AMERICA FIRST

Roosevelt to Give Personal Message In Congress Today

VOL. CXXI, NO. 97 — SEATTLE, MONDAY, DECEMBER 8, 1941 — 5¢ — TWENTY-TWO PAGES

All Military Posts In Seattle Region Go on War Basis

By R. B. Bermann

As swiftly and unexpectedly as a bolt from the blue, war came to Seattle yesterday.

What had been just an ordinary sleepy Sunday morning was suddenly transformed into a day of seething activity with the news of Japan's unheralded attack on Hawaii.

Because Seattle is the center of one of the nation's most important defense areas —and it is in the Pacific Northwest that one of the first blows has long been anticipated in the event of war with the Japanese.

The Seattle office of the federal bureau of investigation also went into action rounding up foreign-born Japanese for investigation.

Both the army and the navy went on a complete war footing.

Here's the way posts in the Puget Sound area were affected:

FORT LEWIS — Post closed to all but essential visitors, and troops with full war packs began moving out to take up positions at strategic points in the Pacific North-

(Continued on Page 4, Column 5)

JAPS DECLARE TWO AMERICAN WARSHIPS SUNK

Also Assert Four Others Are Damaged Together With Quartet of U. S. Cruisers

TOKYO, Dec. 8. — (Monday)—(AP)—The navy section of the imperial headquarters announced today two American battleships were sunk, four others damaged and four heavy cruisers damaged at Pearl Harbor by Japanese naval bombers during the attack yesterday.

The naval statement, broadcast on the Tokyo radio, said there were no Japanese losses.

(By the Associated Press)

TOKYO, Dec. 8 (Monday). —(AP)—Sudden Japanese attacks on American military and naval and island strongholds in the Pacific and on the British bastion of Singapore were announced today by imperial headquarters.

The announcement, broadcast by the Tokyo radio, said the Japanese captured the United States gunboat Wake and sank the British gunboat Peterel. Both were stationed at Shanghai.

Far to the west of that action, the Japanese added, their forces captured the United States gunboat Wake and sank the British gunboat Peterel. Both were stationed at Shanghai.

SINGAPORE BOMBED

Bombing of military objectives at Singapore, Britain's great far eastern naval base, was said to have been executed successfully.

Japanese attacks on the small American islands of Wake and Guam, in the Pacific, also were reported in the announcement.

The first official news that Japan finally had come to grips with the two western powers came in an imperial headquarters announcement at 6 a. m. (1 p. m. Seattle time, Sunday) that a state of war existed with them as of dawn today.

Then Domei followed with a brief statement that naval operations already were in progress off Hawaii, nearly 3,500 miles away, with at least one Japanese aircraft carrier in action against the big American naval base at Pearl Harbor.

Berlin Broadcasts Jap Communique

BERLIN, Dec. 8 (Monday)—(AP) The Berlin radio today broadcast this Japanese communique:

"North American naval and air bases on Hawaii have been successfully attacked.

In Shanghai, Japanese forces cap-

(Continued on Page 3, Column 3)

THE WAR:

Japan assaulted every main United States and British possession in the Central and Western Pacific and invaded Thailand in a hasty but evidently shrewdly planned prosecution of a war she began Sunday without warning.

Her formal declaration of war against both the United States and Britain came two hours and fifty-five minutes after Japanese planes spread death and terrific destruction, in Honolulu and Pearl Harbor at 7:35 a. m., Hawaiian time (10:05 a. m., Seattle time) Sunday.

The claimed successes for this fell swoop included sinking of the U. S. battleship West Virginia and setting afire of the battleship Oklahoma.

From that moment, each tense tick of the clock brought new and flaming accounts of Japanese aggression in her secretly launched war of conquest or death for the Land of the Rising Sun.

As compiled from official and unofficial accounts from all affected countries, the record ran like this:

Honolulu bombed a second time;

Lumber-laden U. S. army transport torpedoed 1,300 miles west of San Francisco, another ship in distress between Honolulu and the coast and sinking of kill another transport, the Gen. Hugh L. Scott, 1,600 miles from Manila.

Shanghai's International Settlement seized; U. S. gunboat Wake captured there and British gunboat Peterel destroyed. Liner President Harrison, now a transport, seized or sunk in the Yangtze River near Shanghai;

Naval Battle Reported In Western Pacific

Capture of the U. S. island of Wake;

U. S. island of Guam bombed, surrounded and oil reservoir and hotel set afire;

Bombing of many points throughout the Philippine Islands;

Invasion of Northern Malaya and bombing of Singapore;

Invasion of Thailand (Siam) and bombing of Bangkok.

The first U. S. official casualty report listed 104 dead and more than 300 injured in the army at Hickam Field, alone, near Honolulu. An NBC observer in Honolulu reported the death toll at Hickam was 350.

The German radio reported that a sea battle between the Japanese navy on one side and the British and U. S. on the other was in progress in the Western Pacific, with a third U. S. warship hit in addition to the West Virginia and Oklahoma.

The British command at Singapore announced the Japanese invasion and said empire forces were engaging the foe.

There was little news of U. S. defensive actions, except the report that a number of the attacking planes at Honolulu had been shot down in dog-fights or the city; an unconfirmed report that a Japanese aircraft carrier had been sunk off Hawaii, and announcement that U. S. army and navy forces had started carrying out secret instructions long since issued to them in event of just such an emergency.

EYEWITNESS ACCOUNT OF HAWAII ATTACK

Waves of Japanese Bombers Sweep Over Pearl Harbor; Parachute Troops Reported

By RICHARD HALLER
International News Staff Correspondent

HONOLULU, Dec. 7.—(INS.)— casualties were reported after two air raids on the Philippine Islands by high-flying Japanese planes, Thomas Worthen, CBS correspondent in Manila, said today in a broadcast from that city.

A broadcast from Manila today said that Japanese parachute troops had been landed in the Philippines.

NEW YORK, Dec. 8 (Monday).—(AP) — At least 290 casualties were reported after two air raids on the Philippine Islands by high-flying Japanese planes.

A flotilla of planes bearing the rising sun of Japan on their wing tips appeared out of the south while most of the city was sleeping. The planes dived immediately in the attack on Pearl Harbor and Hickam Field, the great air base there.

DEAFENING ROAR

There was a deafening roar of explosions.

Three battleships were struck as they lay at anchor in the harbor base.

One, the U. S. S. Oklahoma was reported set afire. Another, the U. S. S. West Virginia, we hear has been sunk alone with another warship.

There was no confirmation of the sinkings by officers of the Fourteenth Naval District.

I saw fifteen planes of one of the sinking group subjected to heavy antiaircraft fire from batteries ringing Honolulu.

Several were shot down around me to aim authorities.

But the report operated through

(Continued on Page 4, Column 4)

Roosevelt Talk On Air 9:30 This Morning

President Roosevelt's address to congress today on the Japanese declaration of war against the United States and the bombing attack on Hawaii and other American bases in the Pacific will be broadcast by all nation-wide networks.

Seattle and Tacoma stations serving as outlets for the networks are KIRO, KOMO, KJR, KOL and KMO. The President's address is scheduled for 9:30 this morning, Seattle time.

Mayor LaGuardia, Mrs. Roosevelt on Defense Mission

SAN FRANCISCO, Dec 7. (AP) Mayor Fiorello LaGuardia, director of the office of Civilian Defense, and Mrs. Eleanor Roosevelt, assistant director, will fly to California tomorrow from New York to aid in organization of civilian defense on the civilian defense coast.

HONOLULU, Dec. 8 (Monday)—(AP)—

The United States fleet apparently has engaged the enemy after Sunday's bombing attack on Hawaii. Destroyers steamed full speed from Pearl Harbor, and spectators reported seeing shell splashes in the ocean. Unconfirmed reports said the attacking planes came from two enemy aircraft carriers and probably these and other ships were being fought by the American ships.

LONDON, Dec. 8 (Monday).—(AP)—Reuters said it was announced officially today in Bangkok that Thailand had ceased resisting a Japanese invasion temporarily and that negotiations were under way.

NEW YORK, Dec. 8.—(Monday)—(NBC)— NBC said today the U. S. aircraft carrier Langley was reported unofficially in Manila to have been damaged in action with Japanese forces.

WASHINGTON, Dec. 8. (Monday). — (AP)—Bombs from Japan made war on the United States today and as death tolls mounted President Roosevelt announced he would deliver in person today a special message to congress at 12:30 p. m. (9:30 a. m., Seattle time).

In the background as the commander in chief prepared to go before the joint session of the house and senate was a government report of "heavy" naval and "large" losses to the army.

Whether Mr. Roosevelt will ask for a formal declaration of war by this country, to match the action taken in Tokyo, was left uncertain after a hurriedly summoned meeting of his cabinet and congressional leaders of both parties tonight at the White House.

Unofficial Reports Hint Major Battleship Sunk

War came suddenly to the United States early yesterday afternoon. Without warning, and while Japanese diplomats were still conducting negotiations for peace, the Japanese air force struck at Honolulu, Pearl Harbor and Hickam Field, all in the Hawaiian Islands. Soon afterward Japanese bombs were raining upon Guam and, later, portions of the Philippines were attacked.

War department estimates said that 104 had been killed on the island of Oahu alone, with more than 300 wounded. Oahu is one of the largest of the Hawaiian Islands.

The reference to "heavy" losses to the navy came from the White House itself, and led some to connect the phrase with recurring unofficial reports that a battleship of the line had been sunk. There were unofficial reports, too, that a Japanese aircraft carrier had been sent to the bottom.

As quickly as word of the first bursting bomb was received, the President as commander-in-chief called upon army and navy to repel the attack.

Tokyo later announced its declarations of war on this country, and Great Britain as well. As was the case here, the British parliament was called into special session for this afternoon.

It was a calm, unhurried capital that went to war today, a capital completely devoid of parades, cheerings and the usual exuberant outbursts of demonstrative patriotism.

WAR EXTRA

BLACKOUT TONIGHT!

RADIO STATIONS TO BE SILENT

WAKE, GUAM BLASTED

U. S. FORECAST: OCCASIONAL RAIN

Occasional rain today, tonight and tomorrow; warmer tonight; fresh and occasionally strong southerly winds.

Temperature at noon today, 47.
Temperature during 24 hours ending at noon today: Maximum, 52; minimum, 38.
Sunrise, 7:46 a. m.; sunset, 4:16 p. m.

Today's Tides		Tomorrow's Tides	
First low	[illegible]	First low	[illegible]
First high	[illegible]	First high	[illegible]
Second low	[illegible]	Second low	[illegible]
Second high	[illegible]	Second high	[illegible]

America's Best Evening Newspaper

The Seattle Daily Times

12 EXTRA

Published Daily and Sunday and Entered as Second Class Matter at Seattle, Washington. Vol. LXIV, No. 342.

SEATTLE, WASHINGTON, MONDAY, DECEMBER 8, 1941. 28 PAGES PRICE FIVE CENTS

TWO BATTLESHIPS, AIRCRAFT CARRIER SUNK, SAYS JAPAN

By Associated Press.

MANILA, Monday, Dec. 8.—The Japanese radio at Taihoku, Formosa, reported in a broadcast today that Japanese warships have surrounded Guam and said all big buildings on the island were ablaze.

Pan-American Airways reported that Japanese bombers "smashed" Wake Island, and that only garbled radio signals were being received from the airways' station at Hongkong.

TOKYO, Tuesday, Dec. 9.—(Official radio picked up by Associated Press)—The Japanese asserted today they had won naval supremacy over the United States in the Pacific, saying by official or unofficial reports the destruction of two American battleships and an aircraft carrier and the damaging of four battleships and six cruisers.

These, declared the Japanese, were the principal results of the first shock of their air-naval offensive.

The assertion of supremacy appeared in a commentary-resume broadcast by Domei, which said that any force the United States now could muster "would be regarded as utterly inadequate to accomplish any successful outcome in an encounter with the thus-far-intact Japanese fleet."

Imperial Headquarters, in an announcement broadcast by Domei, said the two battleships and a minesweeper had been sunk, four battleships and six cruisers damaged, many merchant ships seized and scores of planes destroyed aground and in the air in Hawaii and the Philippines.

The communique said also that a United States aircraft carrier had been sunk by a submarine off Honolulu "although this is not confirmed."

So far as naval losses went, the Japanese said they had escaped unscathed and they acknowledged the loss of only two planes in Philippine actions.

Minesweeper Sunk

The Japanese said that the minesweeper, the 840-ton Penguin, was sunk in an air attack yesterday on Guam, United States naval station.

(An Italian broadcast quoted Domei as listing the 33,100-ton Pennsylvania and the 29,000-ton Oklahoma as lost. Domei also was reported to have said that two United States destroyers and two oil tankers had been destroyed.)

The Imperial Headquarters identified none of the warships reported sunk except the Penguin, but early editions of Tuesday morning papers carried unofficial identification of the two battleships as the Oklahoma and the 31,800-ton West Virginia.

"Observers stressed the magnificent early Japanese success, point out that it was reliably reported that the United States naval strength stationed in Hawaiian waters prior to the Japanese attack comprised approximately 60 per cent of the United States entire naval power," a Domei broadcast said.

"Early losses have reduced the American Navy at Hawaii by two more capital ships, plus a single aircraft carrier, six cruisers (sic)

"Even the addition of the remainder of the United States Fleet to the Hawaiian forces—which is impossible in view of the Atlantic situation—would bring the total strength of the United States naval power in the Pacific to 11 capital ships, 14 'A' class cruisers and six aircraft carriers.

"This force would be regarded as utterly inadequate to accomplish any successful outcome in an encounter with the thus far intact Japanese fleet."

The Japanese spoke little of the first air assaults Sunday on Pearl

(Continued on second following page, Column 6.)

U. S. WAR CASUALTIES

By Associated Press.

The following is the list of members of United States armed forces killed in the war in the East, as disclosed by official advices to the next of kin:

First Lieut. Hans Christiansen, 21 years old, Woodland, Calif., marine aviator, at Pearl Harbor.

Pvt. George G. Leslie, 26, Arnold, Pa., Army Air Corps, at Hawaii.

Robert Niedzwiecki, 22, Grand Rapids, Mich., at Hawaii.

Lieut. James Derthick, 22, Ravenna, Ohio, Army Air Corps at Honolulu.

Second Lieut. Forge A. Whiteman, Sedalia, Mo., Air Corps, at Pearl Harbor. (Trained at Randolph and Kelly Fields, Tex.)

Gordon Mitchell, Hoisington, Kas., Air Corps, at Hawaii.

Pvt. Donald Plant, 22, of Wausau, Wis., Air Corps, at Wheeler Field, Hawaii.

Pvt. Dean W. Cebert of Galesburg, Ill., at Honolulu.

Sergt. James Guthrie, Republican Grove, Va., Air Corps engineer, in Hawaii.

Theo F. Byrd, 20, Tampa, Fla., private first class, Air Corps, at Wheeler Field, Hawaii.

Sergt. George R. Schmersahl, 22, Bloomfield, N. J., Air Corps, at Hawaii.

Pvt. Robert Shattuck, 21, Blue River, Wis., at Hickam Field, Hawaii.

Report of Sitka Attack Unconfirmed

The 13th Naval District said today that it could make no confirmation of rumors prevalent in Seattle that an oil plant at Dutch Harbor was bombed this morning and that bombs had fallen on Sitka.

Many persons, in repeating the rumor, said it had been contained in a radio broadcast. No record of such a broadcast could be found, but one station said it had carried a broadcast here which branded the report as erroneous.

Many Seattle Japanese interned. Following page.

CONVICTION OF BRIDGES REVERSED

By Associated Press.

WASHINGTON, Monday, Dec. 8.—The Supreme Court of the United States reversed today contempt-of-court convictions against The Los Angeles Times and Harry Bridges, West Coast Congress of Industrial Organizations labor leader.

Justice Black, who delivered the majority decision, asserted that the first amendment to the federal Constitution prohibits "any law abridging the freedom of speech or of the press" and "must be taken as a command of the broadest scope that explicit language, read in the context of a liberty-loving society, will allow."

The newspaper was convicted on charges growing out of the publication of editorials about court cases prior to a final settlement.

Bridges was convicted of sending to Secretary of Labor Frances Perkins a telegram, subsequently

(Continued on Page 10, Column 1.)

100 Reported Under Arrest in Tokyo

BERLIN, Monday, Dec. 8.—D. N. B., the official news agency, reported tonight from Tokyo that Japanese officials have arrested 100 persons "of undisclosed nationality" as a counter-espionage measure.

IN THE TIMES TODAY

Amusements	Page 18
Classified Ads	Pages 22, 23, 24
Comics	Page 11
Contract Bridge	Page 18
Dorothy Neighbors	Page 16
Editorials	Page 6
Fiction	Page 16
Finance	Page 22
Marine	Page 21
Obituaries	Page 21
Radio Programs	Page 21
Society News	Page 17
Sports	Pages 19, 20
Strolling Around Town	Page 15
Wirephotos	Page 12

ALL LIGHTS IN N.W. MUST GO OUT AT 11 AS DEFENSE MOVE

Defense of the Pacific Northwest had become so critical late today that Brig. Gen. Carlyle H. Wash, commander of the Second Interceptor Command, ordered a blackout for 11 o'clock tonight from the Canadian boundary to [illegible]

All Pacific Northwest radio stations except Station KIRO in Seattle, were ordered silenced at 7 o'clock tonight. KIRO is to be the mouthpiece of all official news tonight.

The blackouts and radio silence will probably be continued for two or three nights, General Wash stated.

More than 10,000 air-raid wardens, fire watchers, emergency police and emergency fire squads will be at stations or on telephone call in Seattle tonight, Wellington Rupp, chairman of the civilian-defense section here for the State Defense Council, said.

Al Ruth, executive secretary of the civilian-defense section, said 8,749 volunteers were on the rolls eight days ago and that hundreds of other citizens had volunteered yesterday and today.

The city now has more than 6,300 wardens and fire-watchers and about 4,000 others in the system.

The Interceptor Command placed its 6,000 air-raid observers on 24-hour duty at Northwest stations at 1 o'clock this afternoon.

By Associated Press.

SINGAPORE, Monday, Dec. 8.—A report from Manila late today said Japanese forces had made an unsuccessful attempt to land in British North Borneo, but the report could not be confirmed in military quarters here.

By Associated Press.

BERLIN, Monday, Dec. 8.—A D. N. B. dispatch from Tokyo said today that two British cruisers had been sunk in the course of Japanese air raids on Singapore. It quoted a Hanoi dispatch to the Tokyo newspaper Yomiuri as authority.

By United Press.

SAN FRANCISCO, Monday, Dec. 8.—The Singapore Radio, heard by a United Press listening post here today, reported two American-built Hudson bombers operating off the northern Malayan coast had scored direct hits on two Japanese troopships and another Hudson bomber had scored a direct hit on a barge loaded with Japanese soldiers.

MANILA BOMBED TWICE	See First Page Following.
SEATTLE ON WAR BASIS	See Page 9.
U. S. RECRUITING SOARS	See Page 8.
NAZIS MAY AID JAPAN	See Second Page Following.
BERLIN ADMITS RED GAINS	See Page 9.

WELDERS END PEACE CALL, WILL STRIKE

By Associated Press.

WASHINGTON, Monday, Dec. 8.—The United Brotherhoods of Welders, Cutters & Helpers, an independent labor union, today rescinded an order of yesterday calling off a nation-wide strike and instructed all local officers to get their men ready "for a sudden and determined walkout."

A strike set for tomorrow had been called off because of the war situation.

National leaders said the new call came because members of the

(Continued on Page 8, Column 5.)

'We Must Face War United' —Lindbergh

CHICAGO, Monday, Dec. 8.—(AP) Charles A. Lindbergh issued the following statement through the America First Committee today:

"We have been stepping closer to war for many months. Now it has come and we must meet it as united Americans regardless of our attitude in the past toward the policy our government has followed. Whether or not that policy has been wise, our country has been attacked by force of arms and by force of arms we must retaliate. Our own defenses and our own military position have already been neglected too long. We must now turn every effort to building the greatest and most efficient army, navy and air force in the world. When American soldiers go to war, it must be with the best equipment that modern skill can design and that modern industry can build."

NEW YORK, Monday, Dec. 8.—(AP) The American First Committee announced today that because of the United States' declaration of war against Japan, all America First rallies and meetings in the New York area would be canceled "for the present."

Three more Needy Families sold. Music concert nets $492.08. Page 13.

WAR DECLARED BY U.S.; 1,500 DEAD IN ATTACK ON HAWAII

By Associated Press.

WASHINGTON, Monday, Dec. 8.—Congress voted a formal declaration of war against Japan today, after President Roosevelt requested immediate action as an answer to Japan's "unprovoked and dastardly attack" on Hawaii.

President Roosevelt signed the declaration of war against Japan at 4:10 p. m., formally setting the nation to its task of achieving what he called an "inevitable triumph."

A united Congress acted swiftly after the President had revealed that American forces lost two warships and 1,500 had been killed and 1,500 wounded in the surprise dawn attack yesterday. The President asserted one battleship capsized in Pearl Harbor and a destroyer was blown up.

The Senate vote was 82 to 0.

The House vote was 388 to 1. Miss Jeannette Rankin, Republican, Montana, who voted against a declaration of war with Germany in 1917, was the lone member casting a negative vote. Representative Harold Knutson, Republican, Minnesota, who also voted against the 1917 declaration, voted for war against Japan.

Naval Victory Boasted by Japan

As Congress was acting, Japan boasted she had won naval supremacy over the United States in the Pacific. The Japanese asserted in reports broadcast by the official radio in Tokyo, that they had destroyed two American battleships and one aircraft carrier and had damaged four other battleships and six cruisers.

A D. N. B. news dispatch from Tokyo said a United States transport had been sunk with loss of 350 men near Manila.

In his epochal message to Congress, President Roosevelt made no mention of Italy and Germany as he asked for war against Japan.

Both branches cheered to the echo President Roosevelt's

(Continued on second following page, Column 2.)

- - BULLETINS - -

By Associated Press.

WASHINGTON, Monday, Dec. 8.—A White House statement today declared that Germany "obviously" did all it could "to push Japan into the war" in a hope it would end the lend-lease program.

The statement, issued without explanation, said:

"Obviously Germany did all it could to push Japan into the war. It was the German hope that if the United States and Japan could be pushed into war such a conflict would put an end to the lease-lend program.

"As usual, the wish is father to the thought behind the broadcasts and public announcements emanating from Germany with relation to the war and the lease-lend program.

"That such German broadcasts and announcements are continuously and completely 100 per cent inaccurate is shown by the fact that the lease-lend program is, and will continue in full operation."

By Associated Press.

HONGKONG, Monday, Dec. 8.—Japanese planes struck twice at this closely guarded British colony today, running into heavy fire which the British said brought one of the raiders down and scattered the others.

A communique after the second raid declared "the defense plan continues to develop satisfactorily . . . In a raid this afternoon a few bombs were dropped, but the raiders scattered as soon as they were fired on and damage and casualties were not extensive."

In the morning attack nine planes bombed Kowloon, mainland sector of the colony.

By United Press.

MANILA, P. I., Monday, Dec. 8.—Press dispatches reported that 100 to 200 troops, 30 of them Americans, were killed or injured tonight when Japanese planes raided Iba, on the west coast of the island of Luzon, north of the Langapo Naval Base.

By Associated Press.

BERLIN, Monday, Dec. 8.—A D. N. B. dispatch tonight from Tokyo, quoting a report in the Japanese newspaper Yomiuri from Saigon, French Indo-China said a United States transport had been sunk with a loss of 350 men in waters around Manila.

'I ASK THAT THE CONGRESS DECLARE . . .'

TODAY IN WASHINGTON Declaring Japan guilty of a "dastardly, unprovoked attack," President Roosevelt asks Congress to declare war. Listening are Vice President Henry Wallace (left) and Sam Rayburn, Speaker of the House of Representatives. A short time later Congress declared war.—A. P. wirephoto.

KEEP OUT OF THE WAY

In time of war, the military has the right of way. Everybody has a job to do. The civilian can best do his by keeping out of the way of the military—by doing everything he can to cooperate with the Army and Navy. See Page 6 for further editorial comment.

The text of President Roosevelt's message:

To the Congress of the United States:

Yesterday, December 7, 1941 — a date which will live in infamy — the United States of America was suddenly and deliberately attacked by naval and air forces of the Empire of Japan.

The United States was at peace with this nation and, at the solicitation of Japan, was still in conversation with its government and its emperor looking toward the maintenance of peace in the Pacific.

Indeed, one hour after Japanese air squadron had commenced bombing in Oahu, the Japanese ambassador to the United States and his colleagues delivered to the secretary of state a formal reply to a recent American message. While this reply stated that it seemed useless to continue the existing diplomatic negotiations, it contained no threat or hint of war or armed attack.

It will be recorded that the distance of Hawaii from Japan makes it obvious that the attack was deliberately planned many days or even weeks ago. During the intervening time, the Japanese government has deliberately sought to deceive the United States by false statements and expressions of hope for continued peace.

The attack yesterday on the Hawaiian Islands has caused severe damage to American naval and military forces. Very many American lives have been lost. In addition, American ships have been reported torpedoed on the high seas between San Francisco and Honolulu.

Yesterday the Japanese Government also launched an attack against Malaya.

Last night Japanese forces attacked Hong Kong.

Last night Japanese forces attacked Guam.

Last night Japanese forces attacked the Philippine Islands.

Last night the Japanese attacked Wake Island.

This morning the Japanese attacked Midway Island.

Japan has, therefore, undertaken a surprise offensive extending throughout the Pacific area. The facts of yesterday speak for themselves. The people of the United States have already formed their opinions and well understand the implications in the very life and safety of our nation.

As commander in chief of the Army and Navy, I have directed that all measures be taken for our defense.

Always will we remember the character of the onslaught against us.

No matter how long it may take us to overcome this premeditated invasion, the American people in their righteous might will win through to absolute victory.

I believe I interpret the will of the Congress and of the people when I assert that we will not only defend ourselves to the uttermost, but will make very certain that this form of treachery shall never endanger us again.

Hostilities exist. There is no blinking at the fact that our people, our territory and our interests are in grave danger.

With confidence in our armed forces, with the unbounding determination of our people, we will gain the inevitable triumph — so help us God.

I ask that the Congress declare that since the unprovoked and dastardly attack by Japan on Sunday, December 7, a state of war has existed between the United States and the Japanese empire.

FRANKLIN D. ROOSEVELT

The White House

December 8, 1941

The text of the joint resolution Congress adopted, declaring war:

Declaring that a state of war exists between the Imperial government of Japan and the government and the people of the United States and making provisions to prosecute the same.

Whereas, the Imperial government of Japan has committed repeated acts of war against the government and the people of the United States of America therefore, be it

Resolved by the Senate and the House of Representatives of the United States in Congress assembled that the state of war between the United States and the Imperial government of Japan which has thus been thrust upon the United States is thereby formally declared; and that the president be and he is thereby authorized and directed to employ the entire naval and military forces of the United States and the resources of the government to carry on war against the Imperial government of Japan; and to bring the conflict to a successful termination all of the resources of the country are hereby pledged by the Congress of the United States.

The Pearl Harbor Memorial.

BIBLIOGRAPHY

Feis, Herbert, The Road to Pearl Harbor: The Coming of the War Between the United States and Japan (Princeton University Press, Princeton, N.J., 1950).

Hoyt, Edwin P., Blue Skies and Blood: The Battle of the Coral Sea (Pinnacle, Los Angeles, 1976).

Hoyt, Edwin P., Yamamoto: The Man Who Planned Pearl Harbor (McGraw-Hill, New York, 1990).

Ike, Nobutaka, ed. and trans., Japan's Decision for War: Records of the 1941 Policy Conferences (Stanford University Press, Stanford, Calif., 1967).

Layton, Rear Admiral Edwin T., with Pineau, Captain Roger, and Costello, John, And I Was There: Pearl Harbor and Midway — Breaking the Secrets (Morrow, New York, 1985).

Lord, Walter, Day of Infamy (Holt, New York, 1957).

Manchester, William, American Caesar: Douglas MacArthur, 1880-1964 (Dell, New York, 1979).

Morison, Samuel Eliot, The Rising Sun in the Pacific, 1931-April 1942: History of United States Naval Operations in World War II, Vol. 3 (Little, Brown, Boston, 1948).

Reischauer, Edwin O., The United States and Japan (Harvard University Press, Cambridge, Mass., 1957).

Toland, John, The Rising Sun: The Decline and Fall of the Japanese Empire, 1936-1945 (Random House, New York, 1970).

——— Pearl Harbor and Its Aftermath (Doubleday, Garden City, N.Y., 1982).

Tuchman, Barbara, The Proud Tower (Macmillan, New York, 1966).

Wohlstetter, Roberta, Pearl Harbor: Warning and Decision (Stanford University Press, Stanford Calif., 1962).

World War II Flashback   0-681-41181-3 $17.98 Timothy
                                                  Benford
2nd World War in Color   0-681-40768-9 $19.98 Larousse
Also look for these Concise Guides and Concise Color Guides:
Aircraft of WWI & II   0-681-40431-0 $4.50 Jeff Daniels
Modern Civil Aircraft   0-681-40434-5 $4.50 Derek Avery
Modern Combat Aircraft   0-681-40430-2 $4.50 Jeff Daniels
Modern Fighting Vehicles 0-681-40433-7 $4.50 Jeff Lewis
Modern Warships   0-681-40432-9 $4.50 Derek Avery
Weapons of Modern War   0-681-41112-0 $4.95 Associated
                                                  Press
Order by phone with Visa, Mastercard, American Express or Discover:
(800) 322-2000 dept. 706